Apocalypse Countdown 2015 to 2021

Prophecy Codes Signal that the End of Days & Armageddon is Imminent

by Robert Rite

Table of Contents

Chapter 1 - Why the Prophecies are so important today

Many prophetic signs are converging in 2015, making it quite possible that 2015 may be the harbinger year, warning that the apocalypse is imminent. For this reason I believe that this publication is one of the most important that I have ever penned.

Among the many crucial end time prophecies and topics that you will discover are:

- You will discover all of the key prophecies from all of the great ancient prophets
- The key signs of the time of the end
- 2015 - the Harbinger Year
- Where is America in Bible Prophecy?
- The rise of America
- The coming fall of America
- Who is Babylon the Great - America?
- Why will Babylon the Great be Destroyed?
- Who will Destroy Babylon the great?
- How will Babylon the Great be Destroyed?
- Where will the antichrist establish his headquarters
- What nations will comprise the ten nation end time Empire
- Why is Jerusalem such a Burdensome Stone?
- What are the Consequences of Dividing up God's Land?
- The mystery of the Shemita blessings and curses.
- The Jubilee year connection
- The month of September and its link to financial

and national disasters.
- Why there is more to 9/11 than most think?
- The coming seven trumpet judgments
- Who is the Beast of Revelation?
- Who is the 666 - the antichrist?
- Why will so many take the Mark of the Beast?
- The antichrist will come out of which Nation?
- Who are the Kings of North and South?
- Where is "Satan's throne" located?
- Left behind? What the prophecies reveal about the Rapture
- How to Survive the Coming Apocalypse
- Apocalypse Survival supplies and tips
- Emergency Supplies
- How to Prepare Emotionally and Mentally
- And more!

All of the above will be covered, but I will first need to go over some foundational information, that will help you understand the "*why*" about the things that are about to come to pass.

But first let me be very clear that I am NOT predicting that this age will end in 2015 nor am I pinpointing any day, week, month or hour. I will leave the predictions to others.

What I will do instead is reveal signs and unfolding events that make it absolutely possible that the apocalypse MAY indeed begin sometime during this period based on ancient signs and prophecies. Upon reading this book, you will discover all of the signs that point to the later part of this decade (**2015 to 2021**) as the time of the end; and perhaps the beginning of the great tribulation period (the apocalypse).

It is perplexing how mankind prefers to live a life rich in fantasy, theories and science fiction (such as zombie apocalypse), yet at the same time it shuns the non-fiction, especially anything to do with the prophecies of the bible, most of which have already come to pass, save the few which are scheduled to come to pass in the near future. These include the coming one world government, economic and religious system; which we will cover later.

I do believe that as we get closer to the apocalypse, there will be a dramatic increase in interest in the prophecies. Many people will begin to accept that this world is corrupted, spiraling out of control, with a media and government that deceives the masses; so they will yearn to discover the truth. It is already becoming obvious to those who care to listen or watch current events that things are just not right here on planet earth. Things just seem to be getting exponentially worse.

Just as the prophecies warned, in these last days Christians, the rapture and even the name of Jesus will be mocked. This is already the case as the late night network comedy channels consistently mock and blaspheme the name of the Lord. It reminds me of how they mocked Noah as he built the ark in preparation of the great flood. Today, they mock those who believe in the apocalypse and the second coming. The scriptures warn of this very thing in Mathew: *"But as the **days of Noah** were, so also* *will the coming **of** the Son **of** Man be."* **Mathew 24:37**

Despite the many warning signs, most non-Christians and even some Christian people do not know about, or do not care to know or heed the prophecies for these last days. Many will thus be caught totally unprepared, both spiritually and mentally. Here too, I have added a chapter to aid us all in preparing for an impending apocalypse.

Whether you have been a Christian for many years or have attended churches for just a few months, you already know how most churches do not want to discuss prophecy nor anything to do with the apocalypse. Some churches even proclaim that everything in the book of Revelation has already been fulfilled. Whether out of ignorance or not, they are suppressing or avoiding the truth.
Sadly most of the church leaders today do not devote any time to teaching bible prophecy to its congregation, even though the bible is over 60% prophecy. This is because:

1) They are afraid to lose membership
2) They do not understand the prophecies themselves
3) They do not understand the importance of prophecy for this generation

In fact, when asked, some pastors tell their congregation that they do not need to worry about the end of days because they shall be raptured (resurrected) before the apocalypse begins. Others will just say that it is too confusing for them to understand. As you will discover in this book, neither of these may be the case.

Those who have studied and understand bible prophecy all agree that the time of the end is very near. Just like a complex puzzle nearing completion, everything is starting to make sense. All the pieces to the puzzle of the age of man are coming together.

As you will soon discover, very few prophecies need to be fulfilled until the great tribulation period (apocalypse) begins.

Chapter 2 - Birth Pangs of the Apocalypse

In this section I would like to alert you that although we have experienced disasters throughout this age, there is no doubt that the number and intensity of these events have escalated dramatically in this present generation. Many folks blame this trend on global warming, and not the hand of God - as if God cannot control the climate or weather. So Satan once again wants to trivialize God's sovereignty by making mankind think that God cannot control the climate! As I question in a recent article that I wrote in http://Bible-Blog.org ***"Is it global warming or God's warning?"*** There is a clear solution to all of this in the following passage:

"If I shut up heaven that there be no rain (if I send a drought), or if I command the locusts to devour the land, or if I send pestilence among my people; If my people, which are called by my name, shall humble themselves, and pray, and seek my face, and turn from their wicked ways; then will I hear from heaven, and will forgive their sin, and will heal their land" (**II Chron. 7:13-14**).

Natural Disasters - The Signs of the Time of the End

Droughts

There is presently a significant drought in California and other diverse places. According to recent news sources, we are experiencing the worst drought in America in half a century. Dry wells in California are reported to number in the thousands. As a result many California homes have no drinking water flowing from their faucets.

Although we are most definitely experiencing a drought in America, we are not yet in the midst of the global famine that is prophesied for the last days (**Mathew 24:7**).

California drought and resulting crop damages, already in 2014 we are experiencing price inflation on many food items. According to World Bank sources the drought in America could affect prices globally, which would increase the price of food beyond what many people can afford (defined as a famine). From the California fertile valleys to the Mississippi river, the low water levels will continue to increase food price levels here and abroad.

Famine - Food Shortages (11)

While a drought can have drastic or severe repercussions for a local economy, a famine on the other hand is even worse and is defined by Wikipedia as follows: *"A **famine** is a widespread scarcity of food, caused by several factors including crop failure, overpopulation, or government policies. This phenomenon is usually accompanied* *or followed by regional malnutrition, starvation, epidemic, and increased mortality. Nearly every continent in the world has experienced a period of famine throughout history. Many countries continue to have extreme cases of famine."*

In the Old Testament, God promised to bless Israel when she obeyed Him and to curse Israel when she disobeyed Him (**Deut. 28:1-15**). A study of the curses shows that disobedience would be punished by, among other things, hunger and thirst or famine and drought (**Deut. 28:48**). In his day, Isaiah recognized that famine had come upon the Jews as a result of their disobedience to God (**Isa. 51:17-19**). Since rejection of God and His word is one of the main reasons for the apocalypse in the last day, we are warned in **Revelation 6:8** the following:

"When He opened the fourth seal, I heard the voice of the fourth living creature saying, "Come and see." So I looked, and behold, a pale horse. And the name of him who sat on it was Death, and Hades followed with him. And power was given to them over a fourth of the earth, to kill with sword, **with hunger***, with death, and by the beasts of the earth."* **Revelation 6:7-8**

Disobedience to God and famine are not new on earth, but the end of the age will be like the days of Noah when the wickedness of man was great (Matt. 24:37; Gen. 6:5). Then, famine will progress to the point that multitudes will die (Rev. 6:5-8).

When asked about the signs of His coming one of the signs Jesus mentioned is famine (**Matt. 24:7**). He didn't say all of His words will come true except famine. He said His words will not pass away (**Matt. 24:35**). Everything He said will come true including famine. The unsaved will probably blame the famine on Global warming, and the saved will not all agree, but many will rightly attribute it to Global disobedience of God.

In **Revelation 6:5-8** we learn that millions will die in the last days as a result of famine. In another chapter I will show you how God may bless or curse the land depending on our observance of certain land laws that God established (**II Chron. 7:13-14**)

A Global Surge of Great Earthquakes from 2004-2014

There has been an alarming increase in great earthquakes (meaning those measuring 8.0 or greater on the Richter scale) from 2004 to 2014. There have been approximately eighteen of these great earthquakes since December 2004, which is twice the rate experienced from 1900 to mid-2004 (9).

The bible reveals that a great earthquake (or a series of many great earthquakes) will be the final judgment that all but destroys the earth just before the Lord's return. The intensity of this earthquake will be so great that it makes the calamities in the movie 2012 "boring" in comparison. Read it for yourself:

*"And there were noises and thunder and lightning; and there was **a great earthquake**, such a mighty and great earthquake as had not occurred since men were on the earth. Now the great city was divided into three parts, and the cities of the nations fell. And great Babylon was remembered before God, to give her the cup of the wine of the fierceness of His wrath. Then **every island fled away**, and **the mountains were not found**."*
Revelation 16:18-21

Upon reading the passage above, you may be saying "how can every island disappear and the mountains not be found"? Well scientists have discovered that an earthquake that is of a great magnitude and duration can indeed collapse mountains and sink or wash away islands!

Pestilence

An increase in pestilence (viruses and plagues) is prophesied to occur as we approach the end of this age. I am going to address just two examples of pestilence being experienced today:

Tuberculosis

As I write, there are half a million more cases of

tuberculosis worldwide than was previously estimated by the World Health Organization.

The WHO's Global Tuberculosis Report 2014 underscored that the highly contagious disease remains the second biggest infectious disease killer, infecting an estimated nine million people last year and killing 1.5 million.

The new numbers revealed "what many of us had feared, that the TB epidemic is even bigger than we thought," said Dr. Joanne Carter, vice-chair of the STOP TB Partnership Coordinating Board. "This treatable disease is becoming one of the major silent killers in the world," said Dr. Aaron Motsoaledi, South Africa's health minister.

Multidrug-resistant TB (MDR-TB) - the form of the disease featured in FRONTLINE's March film TB Silent Killer, continues to pose a serious threat. This variant of the disease is resistant to two of the first-line drugs used to treat TB. "MDR-TB is much more difficult to treat. It is much more expensive to treat, and there are increased side effects," said Dr. Mario Raviglione, director of the WHO's Global Tuberculosis Program. The problem is that those requiring treatment from the drug resistant form, far exceed the availability of the drug.

Ebola

The first case of Ebola was discovered on 8/28/1976 in a small village in Africa called Yambuku, Congo. At first it was diagnosed as hemorrhagic fever. It was later discovered to be a mutation of the Marburg virus and was named "Ebola". Ebola is named after the river in the Congo where the virus first appeared in 1976. It is believed that the host of the virus is the African fruit bat of Africa. But Scientists are not sure how the virus transmitted from animal to human. There are several strains and the fatality rate can be as high as 90% if untreated. There is currently no vaccine to fight this frightening killer virus.

The Ebola virus (formerly known as Ebola hemorrhagic fever) is a severe, often fatal illness. The illness affects humans and nonhuman primates (monkeys, gorillas, and chimpanzees). It is believed that a person must first come into contact with an animal that has Ebola and from there it can then spread within the community from human to human. The origin of the virus is not certain, but fruit bats are considered the likely host of the Ebola virus, based on available evidence.

People are infectious as long as their blood and secretions contain the virus. For this reason, infected patients receive close monitoring from medical professionals and receive laboratory tests to ensure the virus is no longer circulating in their systems before they can be released. Men who have recovered from the illness can still spread the virus to their partner through their semen for up to 7 weeks after recovery (**17**)

The current outbreak of 2014 began in Guinea West Africa and has spread into Sierra Leone, and Liberia. Once the virus spread to the heavily populated Monrovia Liberia, the virus spread exponentially with 2000 deaths as of September 2014. Since the body is most contagious once the patient dies, the burial process, especially private burials, are a prime source for contamination and the spreading of the virus. Ebola cases in Liberia and Nigeria are believed to be doubling about every two weeks.

In West Africa, Ebola is now an epidemic of the likes that we have not seen before. It's spiraling out of control, and may be getting worse. Today, thousands of people in West Africa are infected. That number could rapidly grow to tens of thousands. And if the outbreak is not stopped now, we could be looking at hundreds of thousands of people infected, with profound political and economic and security implications for all of us.

Pestilences will continue to get worse and more will become afflicted or die in the future with the ride of the fourth horseman of the Apocalypse (**Rev. 6:7-8**). We need to take advantage of every merciful break in between as an opportunity to strengthen our relationship with the Lord, and get our spiritual house in order.

Chapter 3 - Why the Apocalypse?

Upon reading this section, you will discover key reasons why the world will undergo judgment during the tribulation period which is a seven year period just before the time of the end. There are a few other reasons that will be uncovered later, but these are the main ones.

Why will the world go through the apocalypse?

Here are some biblically based reasons:

- To cleanse the earth from all iniquity before the return of Messiah
- To avenge the blood of His saints (Martyrdom of Christians)
- To protect Israel from the invasion forces at the battle of Armageddon
- To punish mankind for rejecting the Lord
- To intervene and end the age of man before mankind can destroy all life on earth
- To reclaim Jerusalem from the hands of the antichrist, and all the nations which invade Israel just before the Lord's return.

Israel and the coming Apocalypse

Many doubters, mockers and even sincere folks alike ask:

"Why would God place so much significance on tiny Israel, one of the tiniest nations and populations on earth, which is hated by so many?"

Many have even rejected the God of Abraham, Isaac and Jacob as the sovereign God because they cannot understand or accept why the God of the universe would place so much emphasis on this relatively sparse ethnic group of people and their tiny parcel of land?

They do not understand how **God many times has and continues to use the humblest of peoples or land** to demonstrate and magnify ***His glory***. They do not understand how God used humble men like Noah, Moses, Joseph, King David, etc. to change the course of history and the destiny of mankind. God does not call upon the mightiest of men (or nations) to perform His service, but rather the meek and humble of the earth so that His name can be glorified among the nations.

The doubters do not understand and or they refuse to accept that Israel is God's land, and its people have been chosen by God as a special people; as His priests by whom God would reach out to the rest of humanity.

Israel is the custodian of God's word, laws, and land as proclaimed by God throughout the bible. It is the land promised to the Jews through Abraham and Moses (**Genesis 22:16-18**). Salvation of all gentiles is from the Jews.

Whether this lost world wants to accept it or not, Israel is God's timepiece for mankind. So instead of hating, or rejecting Israel, and their God, the world needs to understand that what happens to Israel ultimately affects the wellbeing of all nations. We should therefore embrace Israel for what it really is - ***God's present and future headquarters on earth by which all the peoples and all the nations of the world have, are and will be blessed*** (**Genesis 12:2-3**). When the Lord returns to establish His kingdom on earth, the "**New Jerusalem**" will be established in that parcel of land that bears its name.

Understand that when God makes a promise - it is an everlasting covenant that will not and cannot be broken! The land of Israel, particularly Jerusalem is sacred in God's eyes and cannot be bartered away!

Israel, specifically **Jerusalem** is where Jesus Christ died for the world's sins, where Jesus will return, and where Heaven will eventually be headquartered. We read this in **Revelation 21:1-2**:

"Now I saw a new heaven and a new earth, for the first heaven and the first earth had passed away. Also there was no more sea. Then I, John, saw the holy city, New Jerusalem, coming down out of heaven from God, prepared as a bride adorned for her

husband."

Indeed, Israel is God's timepiece for all prophecy and it is the center of the earth - in God's eyes! So God is Israel's defender, despite all of the hatred and contempt that most nations hold against Israel and God! This is why Israel is considered as "trouble" in the eyes of this lost world, and why when the Messiah returns, the one world government of the last days fully backed by a world that refuses to let go and let God **will actually go to war against God, Jesus and Israel (Ezekiel 38)!**

Why Israel is Such a Political Hotspot; a Burdensome Stone

Why is **Jerusalem** called the Holy Land and Cherished by So Many? Why is **Jerusalem** so special in the eyes of Jews, Muslims and Christians? Why has **Jerusalem** become a cup of trembling to most nations of the world? What will this controversy over **Jerusalem** lead to? I plan to explain all of these perplexing questions in this section.

The world has been blinded so that the lost do not realize that this everlasting hatred and or jealousy towards Israel is influenced by the prince of darkness himself who continuously feeds the mind of mankind and its elected leaders with hatred, and confusion. He wants us to focus our hatred on fellow man (instead of on him).   Lies and deception are his primary weapons of choice against his arch enemy; the children of God.

And when the good side wins, then all those who sided with the devil will know who the true Lord is (**Ezekiel 38:22-23**).

Since the Garden of Eden, Satan has tried to circumvent God's plan of redemption for mankind. He is well aware that we were created in God's very image (**Genesis 1:26**) and that we are destined to be kings and priest of the most high for eternity (**Revelation 5:10**)!

The devil knows that *if he can somehow blot out Israel, its land and its people* from the face of the earth, only then might he have a chance at establishing his throne above the true and only God of the universe - the God of Abraham, Isaac and Jacob. He uses nations and world leaders to spew this evil hatred against Israel, Christianity and Jews. In their Satan inspired hatred, they will despise anything related to God, Jesus and the Word until kingdom come.

The enemy in his cunning ways knows that God's plan of redemption for mankind rests on the land of Israel and that this will be the headquarters of the coming new heavens and new earth - Jerusalem. He thinks that if he can conquer Jerusalem that he may block the return of the Messiah. And guess where the antichrist, the leader of the coming one world government will establish his headquarters (for a short time) just before the second coming?

You got it - Jerusalem.

The Holy Land belongs to God!

As already noted, all prophesies about **Israel** and **Jerusalem** which were foretold thousands of years ago have all come to pass, save those that are scheduled for the very time of the end! I do not know of any other book written thousands of years ago with many if any prophecies that have become true. You can decide to believe in whatever book or manuscript you want to, and there are many out there, but I choose to trust the only one that is backed by hundreds of prophecies that have all come to fruition.

Let's consider the mother of all fulfilled Prophecies: After being exiled for 1,897 years, going back to 70 AD Israel once again regained control of **_Jerusalem_** in 1948. This is a big time fulfillment of hundreds of bible passages forecasting such a miracle. Jesus himself forecasted the total destruction of **Jerusalem** that would occur in AD 70. We read about His prophecy in **Mathew 24:1-2** and also in **Mathew 23:37-39.**

Many prophecies including those below make it clear that in the last days, God will punish all the nations for scattering His people out of their land and dividing up the land of Israel.

In Joel 3:2, the Lord says, _"I will also gather all nations...and will pronounce sentence on them_

24

there for my people and my heritage Israel, **whom they scattered among the nations, and divided my land.***" O how the deeds of men* **bring destruction to nations***."*

".....And it shall come to pass in that day, that **I will seek to destroy all the nations that come against Jerusalem***" (Zech. 12:4-9).*

There is no question that what we have just read are serious warnings about what persists unabated today. The nations are still "**hell bent**" on dividing Israel and Jerusalem up for an illusory peace! This peace is an ungodly and unholy kind of "peace", because it violates God's land covenant with Israel, which threatens Israel's very existence, contrary to the will of God.

The Controversy over Jerusalem.

What is incredible to ponder is that **the world consists of 196,939,900 square miles and Jerusalem occupies only 49 square miles!** Yet there is all of this rage, controversy, jealousy, and turmoil over such a tiny parcel of land. In fact, the fight for Jerusalem will lead mankind to the final global war, which will result in the death of billions of souls (yes, and all of this is prophesied in the bible), most will not even know why they went to war to begin with.

As we will learn there is a very sinister plot behind all of this!

There is no place on this planet that is more fiercely contested than those few acres of land located on the east side of the old city of Jerusalem above the Kidron Valley. Christians and Jews call it "The Temple Mount", because that is where the two ancient Jewish temples were located. The beginning of this interesting transformation whereby Jerusalem has become such a holy place goes way back to the time of Abraham.

In **Genesis 22** Abraham is tested into bringing his only son, Isaac, to a place where God commands him to offer Isaac as a sacrifice. God, intervened of course, and personally provided a ram for sacrifice instead of Isaac. The point is the place where God sent Abraham was **Mount Mariah**, which is today called ***the Temple Mount***. Both the event and the place eventually became exceptionally significant for both Abraham's descendants through Isaac, and the descendants of Ishmael (the Muslims).

The Arabs call it "***Haram Ash-Sharif***", because in the religion of Islam that is the place from which Mohammed ascended into heaven. As the dispute continues the weight of world opinion is with the Arabs and they obviously exploit that endorsement at every opportunity.

Prophecy indicates that the third temple will be built on the same spot, by the Eastern Gate (**Ezekiel 43:1-4**), the most famous, but closed, entrance to the mount. Shortly after this temple is built the Lord will return to **establish his kingdom**

here on earth with its center being Jerusalem - the Holy City.

Jerusalem - A Burdensome Stone

The hatred of the Jews and their current control over Jerusalem is the center of the controversy that **Zechariah 12:2-3** and **Zechariah 14:1-3** speaks of reserved for the last days. These verses tell us that ***Jerusalem would become the center of world controversy***. I think you would agree with me that **Jerusalem** and Israel seems to occupy the world news and events so far in 2012 (just like it did in 2011, and so forth).

All of this chaos over Jerusalem is because Satan is working real hard behind the scenes feeding all of the nations of the world an evil delusion which makes many want to blame, hate and attack tiny Israel. This everlasting hatred will only end when the Lord establishes His kingdom here on earth.

These nations have no clue that what they are really doing is siding with the devil in his fight against God, His people, and His land - ***Jerusalem***. None of these nations believe that a devil, demons or fallen angels even exist. They will be seduced by Satan into believing that the destruction of Israel somehow will usher in an age of ***peace***! Satan wants the Jews destroyed because through the Jews God's plans for man's salvation will be fulfilled and they will finally as a nation know Jesus as their Savior.

If Satan can destroy the Jews, he believes it would thwart God's divine plans to return to earth and establish the Messiah's kingdom here on earth through the gateway of Jerusalem. This would give Satan more time to finish off with all mankind.

This is why Jesus prophesied that if he does not intervene against Satan's plan and return when he does, that all mankind would perish. We know that Satan cannot thwart God's plans because God is all-powerful, so he won't succeed in killing off all of the Jews, Christians, and those who attempt to protect God's children, but that does not mean he will not try, and many of God's people will indeed be martyred in the last days.

In Joel 3:2, the Lord says, *"I will also gather all nations...and will pronounce sentence on them there for my people and my heritage Israel, whom they scattered among the nations, and divided my land." O how the deeds of men bring destruction to nations.*

"*I am going to make Jerusalem a cup that sends all the surrounding peoples reeling*. Judah will be besieged as well as Jerusalem. On that day when all the nations of the earth are gathered against her **I will make Jerusalem an immovable rock for all the nations**. *All who try to move it will injure themselves*" (Zech 12:1-3).

Psalm 83 warns all of those nations that continue to threaten Israel in an effort to **"destroy them as a nation, that the name of Israel be**

28

__remembered no more" (Psalm 83:4)__.

The issue of ownership will not be settled until the world learns who God is, when Jesus finally reveals Himself to the world as the King of Kings at His second coming, and that will not happen until the end of the great tribulation.

The Consequences of Dividing up God's Land

The truth of the matter can be summed up very simply: the mount belongs to God not only because He created all things, but He claimed this parcel of land as His. God designated just a tiny parcel of land as His, and He appointed Israel as its custodian, until He establishes His kingdom on earth. He gave it and the entire area to the descendants of Abraham through Isaac (**Genesis 15:18; 17:18-21**). Presently the entire world, including the systematized, organized and self-authorized last-days church recoils at this answer - but God; not nations or man, has the final say. There is a coming **day of vengeance** from the Lord, and we all need to heed His warnings for these last days:

*"…..And it shall come to pass in that day, that **I*** ***will seek to destroy all the nations that come against Jerusalem" (Zech. 12:4-9).***

"Seek ye the LORD, all ye meek of the earth, which have wrought his judgment; seek righteousness, seek meekness: it may be ye shall be hid in the *__day of the LORD's anger__*" (**Zeph. 2:1-3**)."

Jerusalem may be very special for Jews, Muslims and Christians, but this is mostly out of religious and political dogma than anything else; perhaps with a little jealousy, hatred and satanic influence mixed in! *It is special to God, however because it is His land* as the word proclaims throughout the bible. *Jerusalem is where the messiah's feet will touch ground when he returns*! Jerusalem is so important to Satan and all of the supernatural forces and principalities that currently posses this world, because if somehow Satan can take control of Jerusalem, God's holy mountain, Satan believes that God and the Messiah cannot return to reclaim the earth and bring heaven down to earth as promised in the prophecies!

It seems to me that this malignant hatred towards Israel, and this insatiable desire to control Jerusalem is a demonic influence upon all leaders of the world, compelling them to hate Israel and the Jews for absolutely no apparent reason, other than the fulfillment of Satan's wishes to make a mockery of God's chosen people and land, and then from there to attempt to destroy all of God's creation (the earth, animals, vegetation and all mankind)!

Satan's rage will wax very hot in the very last days, as he will know that his reign over the earth will be coming to an abrupt end. So he will take out his hatred and jealousy against those that he hates the most; Christians and Jews. It has been foretold throughout the Bible and make no doubt about it - it will come true in the near future.

The Lord promises to enter into judgment with all those nations who attempt to divide up His Land. (**Joel 3:2**). It is not actually Israel who owns this tiny piece of land, but God Himself. God has assigned Israel as the temporary custodian of His land, to occupy it until God returns to claim it back.

In the last days God says that He *"will make Jerusalem like a cup of trembling to all the surrounding nations who lay siege to Judah. Jerusalem will be like a very heavy stone to all the people, and all those who try to heave it away will be shredded into pieces by the Holy One of Israel."* (**Zechariah 12:3**)

Those who war against the 'apple of God's eye (Israel)' will be ashamed, disgraced, and brought to nothing: *"All who rage against you will surely be ashamed and disgraced; those who oppose you will be as nothing and perish. Though you search for your enemies, you will not find them. Those who wage war against you will be as nothing at all."* **Isaiah 41:11-12**

The Romans in 70 AD, totally destroyed Jerusalem and its temple. They forced the Jews to be scattered throughout the world, and pretty much wiped Israel off the map. Other than Israel, No other nation in history, after having been wiped out of existence, has ever been reborn again!

The Lord foretold this future rebirth thousands of years ago, during the time of Moses! *"The Lord will restore you from captivity, and have compassion on you, and will gather you again from all the peoples where the Lord your God has scattered you. If your outcasts are at the ends of the earth, from there the Lord your God will gather you, and from there He will bring you back. And the Lord your God will bring you into the land which your fathers possessed, and you shall possess it"* (**Deuteronomy 30:3-5**).

Throughout the bible, we read about this miraculous rebirth of the nation of Israel! **In Joel 3:2**, the Lord says, *"I will also gather all nations...and will pronounce sentence on them there for my people and my heritage Israel, whom they scattered among the nations, and divided my land."*

Some immediately protest these bible based claims by arguing that the Abrahamic Covenant has been cancelled either by Jesus death on the Cross or by the Jews rejection of the Messiah. But the Bible clearly teaches that the Abrahamic Covenant is an everlasting one (which means a covenant that lasts FOREVER) and that is still in effect (***Genesis 17:7; 1 Chronicles 16:17-18; Psalm 105:8-11; and Romans 9:4***).

Further, Paul states in Romans 11 that the disobedience of the Jews has not nullified the promises of God to them, *"for the gifts and calling of God are irrevocable"* (**Romans 11:29**). God does not break promises, for he is not like carnal minded man - he is God Almighty!

The Truth behind the Everlasting Covenant

"The LORD said to Abram, "And I will make of thee a great nation, and I will bless thee, and make thy name great; and thou shall be a blessing: And I will bless them that bless thee, and curse them that curse thee: and in thee shall all families of the earth be blessed." **Genesis 12:2- 3**

This is the Abrahamic covenant that established the seed of Abraham, which eventually became the nation of Israel. And to this day, ***those nations that blessed Israel have been blessed and those nations that curse Israel are cursed***.

Many miss the last sentence of the Abrahamic covenant: "in thee shall all families of the earth be blessed". God chose the Jews to be his chosen people not because they were superior in any form or manner to any other race, but because God needed to choose a people and a nation that he could bless **so that through them and their descendants**, all of the peoples and nations of the world would be blessed!

God demonstrated to the world that even though the Jews and the nation of Israel would eventually reject him and the true Messiah, that God would still keep his promise - because God is perfect. God is perfect Love.

The Jews, although scattered throughout the world, because of their rejection of the Messiah, would be re-gathered in the later days to God's Promised Land, through divine intervention, to fulfill prophecy that they may occupy God's land again, just before his return!

By his grace, God gave the Jews the right to occupy and again re-occupy his Holy land, that they may be the custodians of His word (the Holy Bible) and the caretakers of his land until his return.

God Owns Jerusalem and all of Israel!
Therefore, according to the Bible, neither Israel nor any other nation has the right to sell, or divide, or give away any portion of his land, for God Himself holds the title deed (read **Leviticus 25:23**).

So did God make a great Nation out of Abraham?

Were all families of the earth really blessed because of the Abrahamic covenant?
YES! Through the seed of Abraham God not only created the Nation of Israel, but he created a much greater ***"Spiritual Israel"***. Through Abraham, three major religions evolved (Christianity, Islam, and Judaism).

Through Abraham's seed, Jesus Christ the Messiah; the only begotten son of God would be born. He would live a perfect and sinless life, so that he could be that perfect unblemished sacrificial Lamb for the redemption of the sins of all peoples. Through **Jesus Christ**, all of our sins - past, present and future can be instantly wiped clean. Jesus was, is, and shall always be the unblemished sacrificial Lamb of God that wipes away the sins of the world. All those who accept his free gift of eternal life, through his shed blood at the cross, can receive eternal life.

But despite the great blessings that evolved from the Abrahamic covenant, there remains much to be desired in this lost world that we occupy for such a short span of time. Most of the problems throughout the world are because many inhabitants of the world still reject the true God and the Messiah. They prefer the God of this world.

May God protect and shelter all who believe in the Messiah Jesus Christ and in his word in the Bible, from the soon approaching "**Day of the Lord's anger**":

"Seek the LORD, all you humble of the earth, which have wrought his judgment; seek righteousness, seek meekness: perhaps you may be sheltered in the day of the LORD's anger" **(Zeph. 2:1-3)."**

Chapter 4 - Blood Moons, Signs in the Heavens and the Apocalypse

"The heavens declare the Glory of God and the firmament shows His handiwork. Day unto day utters speech and night unto night shows knowledge" (**Psalms 19:1-2**)

This chapter is an excerpt from my book "**Blood Moons Rising**"; updated where applicable. I am including this chapter because certain heavenly signs are occurring in 2014/2015 during God's appointed high holy feast days, which may be a harbinger of significant end time events in the horizon.

The bible does reveal that God provides signs through the sun, moon, and the stars in the heavens?

From the very beginning of this age, God revealed that he created the heavenly bodies not only for the telling of the seasons but also for signs (**Genesis 1:14**). Not only did God provide signs in the heavens as messages for the ancient Israelites, but also to alert and warn us of the impending "***time of Jacobs troubles***" (also referred to as the great tribulation, and apocalypse).

There are six Great Signs in the heavens that already began in 2014 and will end in 2015 that perhaps warn us that the apocalypse may be imminent!

In Luke 21:25 Jesus prophesied that before his return, the following would occur:

"There will be _signs in the sun, moon and stars._ On the earth; nations will be in anguish and perplexity at the roaring and tossing of the sea."
The phrase **"roaring and tossing of the seas"**, refers to the increasing tribulation upon the world such as already occurred in 2014. With the uprising of the ISIS terror group, Russian aggression in Ukraine, another war between Israel and terrorist factions, cyber-terror, demonstrations all over the USA over alleged police brutality among other serious situations in diverse parts of the world, the Blood Moons of 2014 and 2015 may indeed be warning the world about the coming apocalypse!

Key Definitions:

Before we continue, let me offer some key definitions that will aid you in understanding the particular signs that I will cover in this chapter:

Blood Moons: is a total lunar eclipse. It is called a blood moon because of the reddish color that the moon takes on as the earth passes in between the sun and the moon. It is similar to the reddish hue that we observe during sunset.

Tetrad: A series of four blood moons within a relatively short span of time. Prophecy scholars consider this to be a sign of coming events affecting Israel.

Solar Eclipse: A **solar eclipse** occurs when the moon passes between earth and the sun, and the moon casts a shadow over the earth. It is considered as a sign of coming events affecting the world.

God's Appointed Feast days: These are High feast days that God established in Mount Sinai shortly after He declared the 10 commandments. Two of the most sacred are Passover (**Pesach**), and Feast of Tabernacles (**Sukkot**).

Shemita (shmita) year: Every seventh year God had commanded the custodians of His land (the Israelites) that they were not to till or harvest the land - it was to be a Sabbatical year. They would let the land rest and the poor could gather and eat of the abundance of the land, with the promise of an over abundant harvest for the following six years. So if they obeyed this statute they would be blessed. But if they disobeyed, they would undergo judgment.

Elul 29: The climactic last day of the shmita year. It is also the twelfth month of the Jewish civil year. It is a time of repentance in preparation for the High Holy days of Rosh Hashanah and Yom Kippur.

Jubilee Year: At the end of seven Shemita years (7 years x 7) or 49 years, God appointed the following year (the 50th year) as a Jubilee year.

On this 50th year all slaves and prisoners were to be set free, and all debts would be forgiven. Again, the observance of this statute would lead to blessings, and if ignored it would lead to judgment.

The Four Blood Moons - Tetrad

As already defined, a total lunar eclipse is referred to as a blood moon because the event casts a red shadow on the moon. When several (four) blood moons occur within a short period (a two year span) it is called a Tetrad.

There will be a series of blood moons (lunar eclipses), four in all, and two solar eclipses will even be occurring in the midst of the blood moons - all to occur in 2014 and 2015. **The first two NASA confirmed blood moons already occurred** right on schedule on April 15th, 2014 and October 8th, 2014.

These blood moons are all occurring during God's appointed High Holy Feast days. Many prophecy scholars (myself included) believe that God is trying to get the world's attention that something really big is about to happen. I call these divine events: "**signs in the heavens**".

Tetrads that occur during God's appointed High feast days are **very rare.** There have only been **three of these** divine signs since 1492, and after 2015 it is not expected to occur again for 400 years. According to NASA, there have only been about **seven** of these in the past 2000 years.

Let's review what has occurred in the past when these Tetrads have occurred during high feast days. As you will discover below, they seem to usually precede very significant world changing events.

The History of the Blood Moons

32 AD - the astronomical calendar records that a solar and one or more lunar eclipses occurred during the year that Jesus Christ was crucified.

70 AD - the astronomical calendar also records that a solar and one or more lunar eclipses occurred during the time that Jerusalem and the Temple were destroyed.

1492 - A tetrad occurred during Jewish feast days in 1492. In addition to the **discovery of America**, during this period, the **Spanish inquisition** was occurring. The latter led to the torture, martyrdom and expulsion of Jewish citizens who did not convert to Catholicism. Many of these persecuted Jews found refuge in the new world that Columbus discovered

It is believed that Christopher Columbus expedition to discover the new world was financed by King Ferdinand and Queen Isabella with money that they had stolen from the Jews during the inquisition. Oh how the Lord can turn evil into good!

1948 - Four blood moons (Tetrad) next appeared during the time that *Israel was re-established*

as a nation in 1948. By the way, no other nation in history has ever reemerged onto the scene once totally destroyed - especially not with the same name, culture, ethnic roots and people.

1967-1968 - Israel recaptured Jerusalem during this tetrad; after almost nineteen hundred years.

2014 and 2015 - Four blood moons will now happen again during 2014 and 2015! And again, it will occur during God's appointed feast days - clearly a sign from God that we better pay attention because it means that something BIG is about to happen.

Timeline of the Blood Moons

April 15th 2014 - **Blood Moon** (on the **Passover** feast day). This occurred as scheduled.

October 8th 2014 - **Blood Moon** (on the **Feast of Tabernacles**). This occurred as scheduled.

March 20th 2015 - **Solar Eclipse** (during the first Month of the Hebrew calendar)

April 2nd 2015 - **Blood Moon** (on the **Passover** feast day)

September 13th 2015 - **partial Solar Eclipse** (on the **Feast of Trumpets**)

September 27th 2015 - **Blood Moon** (on the **Feast of Tabernacles**)

A **total solar eclipse** will occur in the midst of these 4 total lunar eclipses (blood moons) on **March 20th, 2015**. It is a signal of a significant event that will **impact the whole world**. During 2015 there will actually be two solar eclipses, the second being a partial eclipse, and as will be revealed later both bear significant timing.

The fact that the **blood moons** (total lunar eclipses) are to take place is not as significant as the fact that coupled with **2 solar eclipses** during the same span of time, they will occur during God's **appointed feast days**, and as we will soon learn, they will be accompanied by **even more signs!**

As a result, they may indeed be a great sign from the Almighty signaling that the beginning of the apocalypse may be just around the corner.
Note: the apocalypse is also referred to as the **great tribulation**, the **Day of the Lord's anger**, the **Time of Jacob's troubles**, and **Armageddon.**

These signs may be signaling some other very ominous end of day event(s) that will lead us closer to the **tribulation period** (the last seven years of this age).

As if four blood moons during God's appointed High Feast days were not significant enough, there will also be two solar eclipses in the midst of these 4 lunar eclipses. Yet, as we will soon read, there are two more significant events that will also transpire during 2014 and 2015!

Important Note: The Hebrew month that falls within September and October is called **Tishri**, and it is a very holy month. It begins on a new moon and on a high holy feast day. It contains ten of the sacred appointed feast days that God set forth on Mount Sinai!

Just like *seven* appears to be God's number, *September* (which bleeds into October in the Hebrew calendar) appears to be God's month for blessings and or judgment. And both of these come into play in a big way during 2014 and 2015. *Mere coincidence that the two worst events for America so far this century (as I will soon cover) have occurred in September, and during Shemita years*? I do not think so.

What could all this mean?

According to Hebrew Rabbis, blood moons that occur during high Jewish feast days are usually a bad omen for Israel, whereby *a solar eclipse in the midst of these blood moons, may be **a bad omen for the whole world***.

We are getting a combination of six of these in the span of two years, starting in *2014, and commencing in late 2015*! And as we will discover in the following chapters, there are a few other signs all converging in 2015.

2015 - The Harbinger Year

So is 2015 a Harbinger of Good or Bad news?

That is a **great question**. After all, the events of
1492, 1948, and 1967 were historically
significant and **great news** for **God's elect**. But
has the tide turned? Let's explore this further.

To Hebrew scholars **1998** was a significant year. It
was the Hebrew year 5758. The 5 and 8 add up to
the name of **_Noah_**. They believe it indicates that
1998 began the seasons of Noah, referred to by the
Messiah as follows:
*"As it was in the days of Noah, so it will be at the
coming of the Son of Man."* **Mathew 24:37.**

Keep this passage in mind as we explore events
that have taken place over the past 14 years as we
approach the current blood moon cycle, and we
now explore the significance of the seven year cycle
- the Shemita.

Chapter 5 - The Shemita Blessings and Curses and the Harbinger year -2015

To discover if the blood moons that culminate in 2015, mark the year 2015 as a harbinger of good or bad times ahead, we need to delve deeper into the **mystery of the shemita (also referred to as Shmita).** As we will see, the shmita is a year that heralds in a period of blessings or judgment depending on a nation's obedience to the precepts of the God.

The age of the Shemita blessings

Let's review this term once again. A **Shemita year** occurs every seven years, and it was established by God initially for Israel to allow the land to rest so that it could produce at its maximum potential during the following six year cycle. Just like the weekly Sabbath which refreshes mankind in preparation for the following five or six day work week; a Shmita allows the land to rest for a year prior to the next six year harvest. **It is a time where God blesses or judges nations based on their observance of this and other statutes**.

While some may think that the **Shemita blessings or judgments** were applicable primarily to the ancient Israelites during Old Testament times, this law was never abolished, and is applicable to all nations, **especially** for those who claim that they are a **Judeo-Christian nation** that desires and receives God's divine protection, and blessings.

The Rise of America - Example of the Shemita Blessing

North America was discovered in 1492. Jews and certain Christians (i.e. Protestants) who were undergoing persecution in Europe at the time would now have a bountiful new land for refuge, whereby they could worship freely without the risk of persecution.

America is a prime example of the blessings and greatness that a nation can realize when it's founded under the virtues established by the God of Abraham, Isaac and Jacob. Although today most would never believe this, America was indeed founded and patterned after the laws that God handed down to Moses on Mount Sinai.

America's founding fathers dreamed of a nation that would be the *Israel of the new world*. The Puritans established a day of rest patterned after the Jewish Sabbath, and established holidays also patterned after the Hebrew feast days. Thanksgiving was America's version of the Hebrew feast of tabernacles (Sukkoth).

Many of the Mountains, landmarks and cities in America were given names with biblical roots, such as Mount Zion, Mt. Carmel and Moriah; with cities named after Jericho, Caanan, and Goshen, to name just a few. Yes, just a few hundred years ago most people and leaders in America were spiritually minded and were not afraid to praise God and Jesus Christ in public squares or schools.

46

The founders of this great nation also envisioned a nation founded on the principles of the bible. During his inauguration speech, George Washington dedicated this nation to God and established it as a Judeo-Christian nation, with a constitution following the principles that God set forth on Mount Sinai. America soon became the world leader in spreading Christianity throughout the world, sending forth a myriad of missionaries to all parts of the world to spread the gospel of the Lord.

As a result within a mere 120 years or so of its founding, ***America emerged from World War I as the most blessed and powerful nation on earth!*** Even today, a backsliding America benefits from the overflow of such an enormous measure of blessings; and as of 2014 she is still the most powerful and influential nation on earth by a large margin!

21st Century America in Peril

Now with such great blessings, comes *great accountability* - ***"To whom much is given, much is required (Luke 12:48)***, and now approximately 230 years later, America's spiritual book is deep in the red!

Over the past 50 or so years, America has lost its spiritual and moral compass; casting God out of the public schools and the halls of government, and by creating unrighteous laws and statutes that are contrary to the will of God. She became the premier exporter of pornography throughout the world, among other acts. Our current leader even proclaimed that America is no longer a Christian nation. The USA has de facto rejected the God of the bible; the very God who was and is the source of America's enormous blessings that she enjoyed from her inception.

The Coming Judgment will be Global in Scope

But since this is now a "**global economy**" and America remains a global superpower, the divine judgment that America will receive going forward, will pretty much include the entire world. America's economy is so intertwined in the world that it is like the economic pulse of the world. Just as you cannot destroy a vital organ in a human body and not expect a total systemic breakdown, neither can you destroy a vital nation and not expect terminal consequences for the whole planet.

Note: Keep in mind that America's blessings over the past 230 years or so were not necessarily just a reward from God for our founder's Judeo-Christian virtues, but rather it was the mighty hand of God behind the scenes, influencing events that would fulfill end time prophecies and take us and this world exactly to the point where we are today. Remember that God is always in control, despite how it seems. This is why so many time good comes out of evil (i.e. the holocaust influenced the rebirth of the nation of Israel).

To fulfill the ancient prophecies, God needed Israel to be re-established as a new nation, and God needed a premiere superpower to be Israel's de facto protector (her Big Brother if you will) until the second coming of the Lord!

The 21st century - the age of the Shemita judgments

For the most part the Israel, America and world of today have rejected the **One True God.** So we will now see clear evidence of how the Shemita year has turned from one of blessing to one of judgment. I do not believe that the curse will be lifted unless the world repents; which according to the prophecies will **never** happen. 2015 is the culmination of the next Shemita, and the last two have not been pleasant to say the least!

Something extremely significant has happened in the 21st century. We have all suddenly witnessed how **the first 2 Shemita years of the 21st century have been very negative for America and the world**. Let's review:

2001 - On 9/11 2001 America and the world witnessed the first major terrorist **attack on American soil**. America also subsequently experienced one of the largest stock market crashes in its history. This was followed by a significant financial and economic downturn in America and many parts of the world. It resulted in the war on terror, which persists today.
9/11/2001 occurred during a Shemita year; the first Shemita year of the fledgling century.

2008 - Fast forward seven years later; a financial meltdown occurred in America that almost brought it and the entire world to its knees. It was followed by one of the worst stock market crashes in history as well as a global economic downturn (notice how this clearly affected the entire world - and many parts of the world are still reeling economically from 2008). ***2008 was a Shemita year!***

2015 - seven years from 2008 brings us to the next Shemita year, which started on 9/25/14 and ends on 9/13/15, converging with the blood moon cycle which also concludes in 2015.
It should be noted that the Feast of Trumpets is a day of remembrance and the sounding of the shofar (trumpet) during this holy feast day is ***a call to repentance***.

Two Solar Eclipses in 2015

During 2015 there will also be two solar eclipses.

The **first solar eclipse** of 2015 will be a total solar eclipse and will occur in the midst of the blood moon cycle and right in the middle of the shemita year on **3/20/2015.**

The **second solar eclipse** will be a partial solar eclipse and will occur on **Sept 13, 2015**, which happens to be **Elul 29** which is the climactic last day of the Shemita! The last time a **solar eclipse** fell on **Elul 29** of a Shemita year was in September 1987, just one month later on October 19th, 1987 we experienced one of the greatest stock market percentage crashes in U.S. history.

Folks, the fact that there will be four **blood moons during high Holy feast days**, with solar eclipses of witch the **second solar eclipse** occurs on **Elul 29**, during a **Shemita year,** and all of this occurring in **2014 and 2015**, should get our full undivided attention. As if that were not enough, there is still **even more** that will converge in the 2014 and 2015 timeframe!

The Jubilee Year Connection

As defined earlier, a Jubilee Year occurs every 50th year after seven shemita cycles (7 years x 7). On the Jubilee year all slaves and prisoners were to be set free, and all debts would be forgiven. It must begin in the autumn, on Yom Kippur, the Day of Atonement following the end of the Shemita. Again, the observance of the Jubilee year statute would lead to blessings, and if ignored it would lead to a curse.

Jubilee 1917/1918: The first Jubilee Year of the 20th century occurred in the 1917/1918. What happened during this time?

1) World War I had commenced and America would emerge from **World War I** as the world's premier superpower.

2) The Balfour declaration was signed, which was the first step in the restoration of the land of

Israel back into Jewish hands. In December of 1917 the British conquered Jerusalem and thus in accordance with the laws of Jubilee, the land was relinquished by its occupiers!

1917/1918 was both a shemita and a Jubilee year!

Jubilee 1967: Fast forward 50 years to 1967. This is the significant prophetic year when Israel recaptured Jerusalem in the infamous 6 day war. After nearly 1900 years under foreign occupation, Jerusalem was now back in Israeli hands. Again, in accordance with the law of Jubilee, the occupiers had to relinquish the land. *1967 was both a Shemita and Jubilee year*!

Jubilee 2015/2016: fast forward another 50 years out and it will be the 2015/2016 Jubilee year! So this Jubilee year will follow the year after the blood moons and Shemita year, just as it is supposed to! As we have seen very *significant wars took place* during the past two Jubilee years. So since this trend will most likely continue as we are still under the Shemita judgment, I strongly believe that *a major war* will break out during or around the 2016 timeframe. Could it be war that leads to the *apocalypse (World War III?)*
So let's summarize. In **2014/2015** we have:

1) four **blood moons**
2) all occurring during **high feast days**,
3) a **solar eclipses**,

4) a **second solar eclipse** occurring on **Elul 29**,
5) A **Shemita year**
6) A Jubilee year

If this does not convince you that 2015 will be a pivotal prophetic year - then I do not know what to tell you!

This could be or could trigger the most significant event or series of events in the history of mankind. I truly believe that we are fast approaching the apex of the age of man!

Perhaps the series of blood moons in 2014 and 2015 will fulfill the following Old Testament prophecies...

"The sun will be turned to darkness and the <u>moon to blood</u> before the coming of the great and dreadful day of the Lord." **(Joel 2:31)**

"The sun shall be turned into darkness, and the <u>moon into blood</u>, before the coming of the great and awesome day of the Lord." **(Acts 2:20)**

Now before you conclude that this is all just another false alarm, keep in mind that I am not predicting a *specific* date for the apocalypse. Rather, I

am indicating that most likely what is happening over a short span of time may be a wake-up call from God to all mankind that the **signs of the**

times that Jesus Christ warned the world of in **Mathew 24** - *may indeed be manifesting themselves over the next few years!*

What could it be that these coming great signs are warning against?

Whatever these signs are warning about, most certainly Israel and the Middle East nations will be part of it. Some Christian scholars believe that it may be signaling the **invasion of Israel** by several nations as prophesied in **Ezekiel chapter 38.**

Something will provoke this invasion

Perhaps Israel's enemies feel empowered by the West's continued ambivalence over the ongoing provocative events in the Middle East against Israel and atrocities against innocent civilians and reporters throughout the Middle East.
Could it be provoked by Iran's continued buildup of a nuclear arsenal with the assistance of North Korea and Russia? It could also be a final push to wipe Israel out of the map, as its enemies have been threatening since Israel's miraculous re-emergence as a nation in 1948.

For those who believe in the sovereignty of God and His word, we are reassured by the prophecies

of Ezekiel 38 which reveals who finally wins this cosmic battle between those who steadfastly believe in the God of the Bible and those who harbor an everlasting hatred against God and His people.

As **Rev 19:11-16** promises, God is coming soon to save the world from total destruction and to establish His kingdom on earth!

So let's heed the words of the prophet, and: *"Seek the Lord, all you humble of the earth, who have observed His ordinances; seek righteousness, seek humility; perhaps you may be hidden on the day of the Lord's anger.* **Zephaniah 2:3**

It should be clear to all of us that the signs

discussed in this chapter which are all converging in

2015 are indicating that the period of 2015 to 2021 is pivotal to the history of this age and for the return of the Lord.

The Mystery of the Number Seven and Shemita's influence in the 20th and 21st Century

The **number seven** is God's number, and as you will now see the nations of the world seem to rise and fall in cycles of seven. This is just another example of how the world and everything else revolves around God's mighty outstretched arms.

Even man operates out of this cycle with a seven day week and a median 70 year productive lifespan. So the Shemita is to years what the

Sabbath is to days. The Shemita is God's authority to bless or judge the nations of earth in accordance to their deeds. In this chapter you will discover even more secrets about the Shemita that should send chills up your spine!

The September link to Shemita

The Hebrew month that falls within **September** and **October** is called Tishri. It is the ***seventh month*** of the Hebrew year and it is a very holy month in that most of the high Holy feast days fall within this month! The seventh month seems to work hand in hand with the seventh year - the Shemita. Since the number seven is God's number, the seventh month, September, is God's month to bless or judge the nations! It is the month of repentance and or judgment!

As discussed, a **Shemita** is a sign of a nations covenant with God; and acknowledgement of faith and gratitude for the land and provisions that the Lord has provided. It is a bilateral covenant of sorts. So when that covenant is broken, God who is He that provides our blessings and provisions, has no choice but to remove His veil of blessings and protection.

This law not only applied to Israel but to all the nations and that is another reason why the ***entire world will be subject to judgment during the apocalypse***. But that seems unfair, you might think. Recognize that ignorance of the word of God is a choice, especially when the word is available today in so many different venues. This is why God proclaims: **"my people perish for lack of knowledge"** (**Hosea 4:6**). This applies to each of us as we are ALL His people - created in His own image.

So Shemita is either a blessing or a curse. And the curse can involve not just financial hardships. It can also manifest itself in the physical realm with *destroyed cities* and **collapsed buildings** (as the world witnessed on *9-11*).

The curse will also affect a nation, whom after being greatly blessed by God, rejects Him. America was dedicated and consecrated to the will, word, purposes and glory of God and so it received a special dose of blessings from God. I believe that only 2 nations over the last 100 years fit the bill of abundant favor from God; Israel and America.

America wore the label of Israel, and so the blessings flowed and with it the standards and accountability which applied to Israel would now apply to America. We de facto became the Israel of the new world. Even those Middle East nations that hate Israel acknowledge this truth by condemning both nations equally by labeling Israel *"little Satan"* and America *"great Satan"*.

What these haters fail to see, is that any of the judgments that America may receive will flow through to all the nations of the world as we are all economically connected and all have rejected the God of the universe, in lieu of other gods and idols;

more on this later. Now before I get off topic, let's get back on topic and review a detailed summary of Shemita's influence in the 20th and 21st century.

Summary of Shemita's influence in the 20th and 21st Century

Shemita 1916-1917 - featured a financial crisis, stock market collapse, World War I (which killed over fifteen million people), and the Balfour agreement.
WWI was a very pivotal war which resulted in the collapse of four empires (the German, Austrian, Russian and Ottoman empires). Britain also emerged out of the war in financial ruin. But America emerged as the premier global super power of the 20th century.

1) As discussed 1917 was probably one of the most significant years of modern times for other reasons. It is as if God was giving the world a 100 year warning bell of what I believe will be a climactic period for the age of man - 2016 to 2017 (which will also be the conclusion of a Jubilee year).

2) When America entered world war one, it was a debtor nation; but when it emerged out of world war one it became the world's greatest creditor nation. 1917 was indeed the peak of America's wealth and power.

3) In 1917 it became clear that the center of world commerce had moved from London to New York City and it would remain there for the next 100 years. New York City boasted the world's tallest towers of its time.

Shemita 1930-1931 - during this cycle we would endure the great depression. We also had built the four tallest towers (the Woolworth building, Bank of Manhattan Trust building, Chrysler building, Empire State building), a symbol of our pre-eminence in the world at the time. Towers (tall buildings) are symbols of power and greatness.

NOTE: As a result of the **Twin Towers** collapse on **9/11,** the Middle East now suddenly boasts the largest towers in Dubai and Saudi Arabia! The kingdom tower (which was initially called the mile high tower) is currently under construction and will dwarf all other buildings on earth and it too will be in the Mid-East (Jeddah, Saudi Arabia)! Its final height is still undisclosed.

This could be a sign that the next and *final world empire may have its headquarters somewhere in the Middle East*!

Shemita 1937/1938 - Hitler began his takeover of nations with the annexation of Austria and Czechoslovakia in **1938; a Shemita year. World War II** would commence one year later. Even worse **1938 marked the beginning of Germany's official policy to persecute and exterminate the Jews**. On October 1938 Jewish passports were invalidated and over 1400 synagogues and many Jewish owned businesses were set ablaze and or destroyed on what was termed "**the Night of Broken Glass**". So the Shemita began and ended during one of the worst seven years in human history (1938 to 1944), when all mankind witnessed how evil can reduce nations and men into a demonic entity capable and willing to inflict such genocide upon innocent souls.

No doubt that World War II climaxed by the **Nazi holocaust,** which also ended during a **Shemita year,** was a clear warning; a harbinger to mankind. It was a small taste of the putrid horrors that await an unrepentant world during World War III (the apocalypse).

Shemita 1944/1945 - Obviously **the end of world war two** is the most significant event of the Shemita year of 1945. Fifty million lives were lost in histories bloodiest conflict. Other key events and signs:

1) Hitler committed suicide as he watched his empire, and his visions for a Third Reich reduced to rubble, all within the ***Shemita year*** of 1945.
2) 1945 also saw the **end of world colonialism** (for the most part).
3) The atomic age began in 1945 - the reluctant Japanese empire was threatening to drag WW II past the Shemita. However in 1945, just one month prior to the end of the Shemita year, the USA dropped **2 Atomic bombs** which brought Japan to her knees. Japan promptly surrendered on August 15th, 1945 just before the end of the ***Shemita***!
4) The official end to this horrific war would take

place on September 2nd 1945 aboard the USS Missouri, during the Shemita's last week, within days of Elul 29.

5) On **9/7/1945** the allied armies celebrated their victory over Nazi Germany in Berlin. This date just happened to be **Elul 29** - the very last day of the biblical cycle of seven years the climactic last day of the Shemita! This was the very day of remission, for the collapse of nations, and release of debts! *Still think this is all just coincidence?*

Aftermath of World War II

America had emerged victor after World War I, and after World War II it emerged as the greatest power on earth. After World War II America truly was the epitome of the term "**head of nations**". As noted, 1945 was also a Shemita year! So after 1945 America had emerged as the leader in seven vital areas of power:

1) Financial,
2) Industrial,
3) Commercial,
4) Political,
5) Military,
6) Economic,
7) Cultural
- Her navy patrolled the world's oceans.
- Her currency undergirded the world's financial system
- The fruit of her science, technology, commerce, and luxuries saturated the world.
- She became the world's policeman.

- No other nation came close to her greatness.

During the **1951-1952** and **1958-1959** Shemita years American continued to bask in its financial and military prowess.

Shemita 1965-1966 - reeling from the assassination of JFK in 1963, America enters the Vietnam War in 1964. This would be the first major war that America would lose.

The groundbreaking of the World Trade Centers also began in 1966, but these towers just like the hope for victory in Vietnam would eventually collapse. Had the cycle of the Shemita Blessings for the USA been broken as early as 1965? Let's continue on with the next cycles and see.

Shemita 1973-1974 - When a nation is under judgment, every 28 years (which is a cycle of 4 Shemita years) that nation experiences some form of defeat.

1) Twenty eight years after the apex of America's unquestionable power in 1945, we arrive at 1973. In 1973 after failing to accomplish its mission, the last US troops withdrew from Vietnam. This was the first major war that America had lost.

2) Facing impeachment Richard Nixon resigned in disgrace on August 9th 1974, just one month before the end of the Shemita year which ended in September 1974.

3) The World Trade Centers were also completed in 1973. Note that twenty eight years later in 2001 the Twin Towers would collapse; in **28 years - 4 Shemita cycles of 7 years each; clearly a divine sign of Judgment!**

4) In 1973, Roe vs. Wade set the stage for legalizing abortion.
As noted, 1973 was also the beginning of the Shemita year 1973/1974.

So, facing political and military embarrassment in 1973/1974, for the first time in nearly a century, the Shemita blessings upon America now seem to have run their course and clearly signal a reversal of fortunes upon this great nation.

But Why?

Well let's take the two most fateful moral and spiritual decisions that America made in the twentieth century:

1) In the 1960's America began its campaign of banning God and His word from all public places and schools.

2) In 1973, the courts under Roe vs. Wade, ruled for legalizing abortion. Since that fateful decision **over fifty million babies (considered as saints in God's eyes)** have been aborted. This was a turning point whereby the highest court of the land made it legal for mankind to make decisions over the sanctity of life, over and above the will and the commandment of God (**thou shall not kill**). It marked the beginning of the great moral decline of America.

As we will now see the Shemita years for America from this point forward appear to be judgment based, a reversal of the Shemita blessings bestowed upon the USA throughout the first sixty years or so of the twentieth century.

Shemita 1979-1980 - USA recession; US Embassy captured in 1979.

Shemita 1987 - stock market crash (Black Monday)

Shemita 1994 - Market correction

With the blessings come the curse - if a nation who seeks and receives the Lord's blessings subsequently rejects Him, and then He will remove the blessings and her veil of protection.

9/11 America's Great Day of Shaking

Shemita 2000-2001 - 9/11/2001 was one of the darkest days in American history. It can be likened to the Japanese attack on Pearl Harbor. Targeting the Twin Towers was very strategic in that by doing so, the enemy was attacking America's symbol of global financial dominance. The World Trade Centers were symbols of wealth and money - with the two imposing monuments which became symbols of the god of money and wealth that the nation increasingly worshipped. As you will discover below, **9/11** was a very prophetic end time event.

In addition to the collapse of the towers, when the stock market finally opened six days later on 9/17/2001, it was incredibly the final day of the Shemita which had started on September 30, 2000 and ended on September 17th 2001!

The date of 9/11 was the climactic end and also biblical month of Tishri, and Elul 29; the ***biblical day of financial nullification***. The latter actually ended on 9/17/2001. It was the date that the financial markets reopened and closed that day with one of the worst stock market crashes ever - fulfilling the financial nullification on that exact day.

So the **Twin Towers were consummated, begun, completed and eventually totally destroyed in one 28 year cycle consisting of four separate seven year Shemita periods!** This is obviously **NOT coincidence** but a clear sign from God.

The Significance of the Twin Towers of the World Trade Centers

Towers are symbols of power and greatness. However when a nation does not give the glory to God, they become prideful and then the towers bring forth the curse of Babel (**Genesis 11:1-9**); and the same judgment that befell the Tower of Babel, also applied to the twin towers when they also fell. God warns us that He will bring down the lofty in **Isaiah 2:12-15**. This is why when a nation is under judgment its towers may also fall.

So if the rising of towers can be linked to the apex of a nation's prosperity and might, so then the collapse of its towers may mark the fall of that nation.

Today, even after construction of the new world trade center, the tallest buildings are no longer in America. They are in the Middle East (Dubai and Mecca). So if towers are an indication of nation's blessings, then when they fall it may signal the beginning of that empires demise, and its replacement with a new empire. It is as if the mantle of the symbol of towers has changed hands from America to the Middle East. So will the last empire (the beast nation that will rule the world) have its headquarters somewhere in the Middle East?

This scenario makes sense since Satan would do anything to take over the Middle East in a vain attempt to prevent or delay the return of the Messiah which most Christians know will take place on Mount Zion in Jerusalem; the area where the Messiah was crucified and subsequently resurrected! His is also the most controversial and sacred parcel of land in the world!

Shemita 2007-2008 - Seven years later takes us to the 2007-2008 Shemita year. No blessings here either folks! A Global Financial meltdown which originated in America spreads throughout the world.

In 2012 - as the new tower was being completed on ground zero (as if an omen upon the pagan nations of the world), there was a **solar eclipse** on the exact day the spire was set atop the tower!

Shemita 2014-2015 - Began on September 24th, 2014 and ends on September 13th, 2015. The climactic day, Elul 29, the day of remission, will fall on Sunday, September 13th, 2015 (a Sunday).

9/11/2015 will be the last day the market is open before Elul 29 - just like on 9/11/2001. There will be 2 solar eclipses in 2015, in the midst of Shemita, and the second one will occur on Elul 29 (9/13/2015).

Other Interesting Points about Shemita, Elul 29 and Tishri

Elul 29 - Is the month that leads into and builds up to the Shemita's beginning and end. When it occurs at the end if a Shemita year, it is a biblical day of **financial collapse**, where the slate is wiped clean and financial accounts are wiped away. It is the day of cancelling one's debts, one's credits, remission and nullifying financial accounts.

Tishri - Is the first month of the Shemita year?

Wake - Is the climactic 7 year end of the Shemita

Why care?

Well **60%** of the greatest stock market crashes have occurred during or within just one week of *Tishri*. **75%** of all stock market crashes have occurred during Shemita years! Also, the three greatest stock market crashes in history all occurred on **Tishri** and each took place on the Shemita climactic conclusion or wake.

Timeline to the Apocalypse

The tribulation (apocalypse) could begin sometime right after 2015. Seven Shemita years x seven is 49, the 50th year being a Jubilee year. Add fifty years to 1967 and it brings us to the 2016/2017 Jubilee year. This makes sense since the Shemita has not been observed in Israel or anywhere else in the world since 1967 - releasing Judgment or a curse for this period.

Is there hope for America and the world?

God is sovereign so that if nation(s) repent judgment can be cancelled or pushed out. However *you and I know* that there has been no repentance or spiritual revival anywhere in site during the 21st century. **The coming apocalypse is therefore all but certain;** save that God in His mercy could delay it all if He so chooses.

Mystery of the Darkening of the Sun

As indicated previously, solar eclipses can be a sign of judgment upon the nations, financial and otherwise. Below are some key events associated with solar eclipses.

The New Tower at Ground Zero: Many people are not aware that at the time the new tower at ground zero was completed, and the finishing spire was put in place, there was a solar eclipse (**April 29th**). There may be a sign associated with the timing of solar eclipse and completion of the new tower; which remains to be seen.

9/12/1931 - a solar eclipse occurred on this date. It was the end of the Shemita year (Elul 29 - last day of Shemita associated with financial nullification). Within a month or so Wall Street and other markets throughout the world experienced the worst stock market crash in its history.
9/23/1987 - a solar eclipse occurred on 9/23/1987 also on Elul 29 thirty days later Wall Street experienced one of the worst stock market crashes in its history which was referred to as "**black Monday**".

2015 Eclipses: There will be two of these solar eclipses in 2015 in the midst of the Shemita year.

- The first will occur on March 20th, 2015 smack in the mid-point of the Shemita year, and commemorating the beginning of the Holy feast days starting with Nisan.

- The **second solar eclipse of 2015** will take place on **September 13, 2015, on Elul 29. This will be** the last day of the Shemita year, the day of financial nullification. The last times this occurred were in 1931 and 1987, as noted above both of these signs were followed by significant stock market corrections, with the former occurring at the beginning of the great depression, with the deflationary spiral beginning in 1931.

The Jubilee Signs

So every 7 days is a Sabbath day, every 7 years is a Shemita year, and every 7 Shemita's (49 years) is followed by a Jubilee year. Since the Jubilee year follows the Shemita it is celebrated on the 50th year. It was the year of liberty when all slaves were set free. It was the year or return, reconciliation, and the restoring of land back to its rightful owner.

The Restoration of Israel

NOTE: AD 70 was also a Jubilee year, and in this case Israel was under judgment for the rejection of their Messiah Jesus Christ. So the Jubilee of AD 70 was not one of celebration, but of mourning over the judgment. However 1,847 years later the events leading to the re-establishment of the nation of Israel would begin. Let's read.

1917 - Was a significant prophetic year with regards to the Jubilee, Israel, and end of day prophecies. This year consisted of the end of the

Shemita and the beginning of the Jubilee (Both on 9/16/2017). So when British Field Marshall Edmund Allenby marched into Jerusalem and liberated it on 12/11/1917 from the Ottoman Empire. It was a Jubilee year, the year of reconciliation where land is restored to its owner - in this case the occupier was ousted from Jerusalem.

1967 - The next Jubilee year would occur **50 years** later from **1917 to 1967**. Once again a very significant and prophetic restoration occurred when Jerusalem was restored back into Israel hands. While other nations may have called this day a great catastrophe, to the Hebrews, Christians, and all who understand and believe in prophecies in the bible it is a great event. In 1967 Jordan relinquished Jerusalem and it was restored in the year of restoration back to Israel! Israel was dispossessed of its land approximately 1900 years earlier when the Roman Empire destroyed Jerusalem in AD 70. The Romans subsequently **changed the name of Israel to Palestine**.

Jubilee Sept. 2015 to Sept. 2016 - The next Jubilee falls in the period 9/2015 to 9/2016, immediately following the end of the Shemita year of 9/2014 to 9/2015. Interesting to note that the last two Jubilees occurred during wars, World War I and the Six-Day war. If this trend continues, as I believe it will, we can then expect a major war in the 2015-2016 timeframe. **Could it be the beginning of World War III (the apocalypse)**?

So in 2014/2015 we have 4 blood moons - 2 Solar Eclipses - a Shemita year, followed immediately by the Jubilee year of 2015/2016. If this is not a climactic set of divine dates - then I do not know what is!

Chapter 6 - Timeline to the Apocalypse

Prophecies that have already been fulfilled

I think it is appropriate to begin with key end time prophecies that have already been fulfilled since they were intended for Israel and the Hebrews in their formative years. But a healthy percentage of all prophecies are intended for our generation in these last days. It stands to reason that God would want our generation to heed the warning signs for these last days, since the population of this earth is at around seven billion souls, more than any other time period throughout the age of man.

Since the prophecies in the bible thus far have all come to fruition, this fact alone should lend credence to the belief that all of God's elect hold, and this is that the bible is the infallible and or inspired word of the God of the universe. There is no doubt from the scriptures that God wants to reveal many future events to us.

Isaiah 46:10a-11b; Amos 3:7 and Mathew 24:15 all reveal that God wants us to figure out the future of mankind through the prophecies.

In the book of Luke, we read an example of a prophecy that was fulfilled after Jesus death. In **Luke 19:41-44** Jesus who obviously already knew this, prophesied how the Jews would reject him and how as a result Jerusalem would be destroyed in 70 AD and the Jews would be dispersed throughout the nations.

Seven Prophetic events of the Apocalypse

Prophecy scholars agree that there are seven major prophetic signs for the Second Coming (1). The first two have already been fulfilled. The other five will be revealed in the following section.

1. Israel will re-emerge as a Nation... (Ezekiel 36:8-12, 37:21)

This prophecy was fulfilled in 1948. Although Israel ceased to exist altogether after AD 70, she reemerged in 1948 again as a nation, after 2,000 years! No other nation in history has re-emerged after having been totally destroyed, and its people ejected from their land. No other people have been able to retain its heritage, culture, Jesus declared in **Mathew 24:34**, that generation that witnesses the rebirth of Israel will be the people that shall witness the end of this age and the return of Messiah. A generation is 70 years, so if we add 70 years to 1948 we arrive at 2018! 2018 is within the timeframe of 2015 to 2021 which is the period that I believe may herald in the Apocalypse. Granted there may be some wiggle room here, as the lifespan of man has increased over the past one hundred years or so; but as always God is in control and He determines when the hammer will drop.

God declares: "You, O mountains of Israel, will produce branches and fruit for my people Israel, for they will soon come home. I am concerned for you and will look on you with favor; you will be plowed and sown, and I will multiply the number of people upon you, even the whole house of Israel. The towns will be inhabited and the ruins rebuilt. I will increase the number of men and animals upon you, and they will be fruitful and become numerous. I will settle people on you as in the past and will make you prosper more than before. Then you will know that I am the LORD. I will cause people, my people Israel, to walk upon you. They will possess you, and you will be their inheritance; you will never again deprive them of their children."

This is what the Sovereign LORD says: I will take the Israelites out of the nations where they have gone. I will gather them from all around and bring them back into their own land.

2. Israel will recapture Jerusalem (Luke 21:24)

This prophecy was fulfilled in 1967, when Israel recaptured the entire city.
"They will fall by the sword and will be taken as prisoners to all the nations. Jerusalem will be trampled on by the Gentiles until the times of the Gentiles are fulfilled." **Luke 21:24**

One can say that **1967** was the end of or the winding down of the "time of the gentiles". This major prophetic event is also another major sign that this is the generation that witnesses the time of the end.

Clearly Satan does not want Israel to be in the hands of Jerusalem because he knows that this is ground zero for the return of Messiah. The end time prophecies clearly reveal that the Messiah will establish His kingdom in a revamped "**New Jerusalem**" (**Revelation 21**).

This explains why Satan has influenced the minds of almost every leader of the gentile nations with a relentless desire to divide Jerusalem. The media also seems to want to blame Israel for any violence in the area, even when it is clear that Israel is merely defending itself or retaliating against its aggressors. Even sadder is how the masses fall for this clear demonic deception!

Also unexplainable is how mankind fails to recognize how Israel is in itself a miracle and how Gods hand is clearly involved in Israel's survival and blessings given that despite its tiny size and population, it commands the attention, hatred and fear of the entire world day in and day out! This also is a clear fulfillment of **Zechariah 12:2-3 (and other verses)** which prophesy that Israel would become a trembling cup, immovable rock and burdensome stone to the world during the time of the end. As we will cover in the next major event that follows, certain prophecies are also very clear that those nations that persist in dividing up God's land are playing with fire, literally!

What must happen next - twelve key Events to take place during the Apocalypse

Below is my timeline of events that are still to take place based on the prophecies of Daniel, Ezekiel, Revelation and other end time prophets. Keep in mind that while the twelve key end time events unfold, the world will be enduring great tribulation through relentless worldwide catastrophes, famine and the like, which will be uncovered in a later section.

1) A Coalition of 10 nations will form **(Rev. 13)**

2.a) The identification and rise of the man of perdition; aka antichrist **(Rev. 13)**
2.b) Establishment of the beast kingdom - one world Government **(Rev.13)**

3.a) Creation of the one world religion **(Rev. 13)**
3.b) Antichrist will enforce the worship of only him as god.

4) The antichrist will establish a seven year peace treaty with Israel, permitting her to rebuild the Jewish Temple.

5) The two witnesses **(Rev. 11)** will emerge on the scene and usher in a great revival. The 144,000 are anointed **(Rev. 7)**

6) Persecution of the Saints **(Rev. 12).**

7) Abomination of Desecration

8) Destruction of Babylon the Great **(Rev. 18)**

9) Rapture of the body of Christ **(the elect)**

10.a) Battle of Armageddon **(Ezekiel 38:2-6)**
10.b) the "Great Day of God Almighty" **(Rev. 16)**

11.a) Return of the Messiah **(Rev. 19:11-16)**
11.b) Satan and his followers are captured, and judged at the "Great White Throne Judgment" **(Rev. 20)**

12) A New Heaven and New Earth for eternity (Rev. 21-22)!

Now we'll explore some of the above key events in further detail. The following is additional information, supporting passages and possible scenarios for some of these twelve key Events to take place during the Apocalypse.

1) Ten Nations will unite to form the "Beast kingdom" of Rev 13 and 17:9-10

This prophecy has yet to play out, although the beast kingdom could spring up rather quickly once the opportunity avails itself in the form of some calamity or other global crisis. Many prophecy scholars believe that this passage infers that the Roman Empire will once again emerge as the last kingdom on earth; referred to as the "beast kingdom" under the control of the man of perdition (the antichrist).

"This calls for a mind with wisdom. The seven heads are seven hills on which the woman sits. They are also seven kings. Five have fallen, one is, the other has not yet come; but when he does come, he must remain for a little while." **Rev. 17:9-10**

Although it is **NOT likely** that **Rome** will suddenly emerge and grow into this powerful world dominating empire, I believe that Revelation 13 and 17 uses Rome symbolically, inferring that the beast kingdom will have the type of economic, and military prowess that the Roman Empire enjoyed at the time that John penned Revelation. Other possibilities include:

- Rome as part of the E.U
- A coalition with headquarters in any one of the Muslim nations that the Roman Empire once occupied; this scenario is referred to as a "Mid-East Beast".

As will be discussed later, I believe the second scenario will be the most likely connection to the Roman Empire of the first century AD.

3.a) The One World Religion (Rev. 13:8)

This prophecy cannot be fulfilled until the beast kingdom is formed, since the one world religion will be enforced once the man of perdition is identified and reigns.

"All inhabitants of the earth will worship the beast- all whose names have not been written in the book of life belonging to the Lamb that was slain from the creation of the world." **Rev. 13:8**

Some believe that the one world religion will be the Roman Catholic Church based in the Vatican, because they believe that the Roman Empire will rise up once again.

Much more likely, I believe that it will be a pagan religion composed of several major religions. This scenario makes sense because the Babylon religion of the last days is referred to as a **_"harlot"_** (a prostitute), inferring a religion that worships many gods. In the Old testament God refers to those who worship multiple idols, and gods as "**playing the harlot**" and engaging in "**fornication**". Here are just two passages that explain this:

*"So it came to pass, through her casual **harlotry**, that she defiled the land and committed adultery with stones and trees."* **Jeremiah 3:9**

*"Then those of you who escape will remember Me **among the nations where they are carried captive**, because I was crushed by their adulterous heart which has departed from Me, and by their eyes which **play the harlot** after their idols; they will loathe themselves for the evils which they committed in all their abominations."* **Ezekiel 6:9**

*"...She will return to her hire, and commit **fornication** with all the kingdoms of the world on the face of the earth."* **Isaiah 23:17**

3.b) The leader of the One World Government will Claim that he is god and will force the mark of the beast - and will Martyr Christians and Jews (Rev 13:6-8)

So just before the apocalypse, a charismatic person will emerge on the scene that will seem to have all of the answers to the world's woes. Thus he will quickly gain control of the world's political, military, and economic machine. Then he will establish a one world religion whereby he will eventually require all to worship him as god!

The worship of the beast will occur by the middle of the tribulation period, three and one half years after the antichrist confirms a seven year peace treaty with Israel. By the mid-point of the seven year tribulation period the whole world was astonished and followed the beast.

Men and nations are easily swayed by their leaders. They place too much trust on their elected officials. Usually all it takes is a person with presence, charisma and wit, to win the hearts and worship of the masses. We saw this with Hitler in Germany and we will see it again when the man of perdition comes on the scene.

It is very disturbing to witness how easily a whole nation can be manipulated into a state of panic and fear. I recall how on September, 2014 the whole nation was gripped in fear over the death of one Ebola victim. The Media ran the story endlessly for about one week. The stock market began to crash and airlines were reporting a drop in passenger loads. Yet within just one week or so everything seemed to be back to normal as if nothing ever happened - and the media suddenly stopped reporting on the virus, even after the second Ebola death. It is as if the inhabitants of the earth are being conditioned to be swayed in different moods or direction depending on how the government and the media want them to.

More on this in the chapter titled: **"The 666 - the Man of Perdition".**

8. "Babylon the Great" will be Destroyed (Rev. 18:8-10)

This key event will not be fulfilled until the beast kingdom is financially, militarily and politically ready to control the world. The beast kingdom which will reign under the control of Satan will only be able to reign supreme by taking out a great nation reigning at the time of the end. That great nation is referred to as *"Babylon the Great"*. **Revelation 18** declares that this great nation will be utterly destroyed in just one hour. Let's read some key passages:

*"Therefore her plagues will come in one day—death and mourning and famine. And **she will be utterly burned with fire**, for strong is the Lord God who judges her.*
*The kings of the earth who committed fornication and lived luxuriously with her will weep and lament for her, when they see the smoke of her burning, standing at a distance for fear of her torment, saying, 'Alas, alas, that great city Babylon, that mighty city! For in **one hour your judgment has come**."* **Rev. 18:8-10**

More on this important event in the chapter titled: **"Who is Babylon the Great?"**

10.a) The Battle of Armageddon

A Moslem Coalition which may also include

Russia and other Asian nations, invades Israel (Ezek. 38:2-6)

This prophecy of the "battle of Gog/Magog" has yet to be fulfilled, as it will occur just before the Lord's triumphant return.

"Son of man set your face against Gog, of the land of Magog, the chief prince of Meshech and Tubal; prophesy against him. This is what the Sovereign Lord says: I am against you, O Gog, chief prince of Meshech and Tubal. I will turn you around, put hooks in your jaws and bring you out with your whole army-your horses, your horsemen fully armed, and a great horde with large and small shields, all of them brandishing their swords. Persia, Cush and Put will be with them, all with shields and helmets, also Gomer with all its troops, and Beth Togarmah from the far north with all its troops-the many nations with you." **Ezekiel 38:2-6**

In fact, **Rev. 19:19-21** reveals how in the last days many nations will side with the devil (whether knowingly or ignorantly) and form a coalition that will invade Israel just before the Lord's return. These world leaders, presidents and kings fail to understand that all of the nations that engage in the invasion of Israel in the final battle just before the Lord's return - will be utterly defeated by God Himself (**Ezekiel 38:22-23**).

"And I will bring him to judgment with pestilence and bloodshed; I will rain down on him, on his troops, and on the many peoples who are with him,

flooding rain, great hailstones, fire, and brimstone. **23** *Thus I will magnify Myself and sanctify myself, and I will be known in the eyes of many nations. Then they shall know that I am the Lord."* **Ezekiel 38:22-23**

So as is the case today, the gentile nations will continue to meddle in the affairs of Israel and continue to deny its right to defend itself and to pressure her into dividing up her land even more than it already has, until it is incapable of defending her territory. This will persist until the invasion of the battle of Armageddon and the return of the Messiah **Daniel 2:36-45; Zech. 14:2; Rev. 11:1-2**.

Signs in the Heavens - the Harbinger for the Apocalypse?

 2014-2015 - The four blood moon (total lunar eclipses) signs commenced in 2014, with the first two having occurred right on schedule. In addition to the blood moons a few other significant prophetic signs and events are also schedule to conclude or commence in 2015.

Based on ancient Hebrew teachings, these blood moon signs among the others are signaling that something very big is about to happen to Israel and to the world.

2014

- **Blood Moon** on April 15th 2014
- **Blood Moon** on October 8th 2014

2015

- **Blood Moon** on April 4, 2015 - on the first day of Passover (visible in: Asia, Australia, Pacific, Americas).
- **Blood Moon** on Sept. 28, 2015 - First Day of Sukkot (visible: Eastern Pacific, Americas, Europe, Africa, and Western Asia).

Other significant dates in 2015:
- The **Shemita**, a seven-year cycle that began on Rosh Hashanah on Sept. 30, 2008, ends on Rosh Hashanah on Sept. 13-14, 2015. The sabbatical year from 2014 ends here, too.
- **Solar Eclipse** on Sept. 13, 2015 (Elul 10, 5776), on Rosh Hashanah.
- **Jubilee year** begins on Sept. 23, 2015 (Elul 20, 5777) on Yom Kippur.

These signs and several other signs that will all be converging in 2014 and 2015 are covered in much more detail in the following chapter.

Chapter 7 - The Book of Revelation and the Apocalypse

While the prior chapter was date specific relative to heavenly signs and appointed feast days that could be harbingers of the apocalypse. We will now discover the events and the series of judgments that will unfold once the apocalypse begins.

The book of Revelation is appropriately the last book of the bible, because it is primarily the **go to book on the last days of this age**. It also is the revelation of Jesus Christ in that it reveals that Jesus Christ was and is the Messiah, and He will return to rule the world at the conclusion of this age of man. God allowed man 6,000 years to mess everything up and prove that **without the Spirit of God** mankind has always and will always be unable to resist the temptations of their carnal spirit which makes them susceptible to the cunning of Satan and his dark evil influences, which has and will ultimately lead this world to its demise.

To stay in topic let's review the key clues in the book of Revelation regarding the apocalypse and what types of events are revealed to take place before during and after the great tribulation period (apocalypse).

The apostle John was in exile in the Island of Patmos by the Romans because of his testimony of Jesus. While in exile, he received many visions from Jesus and some of His angels. John could only describe these visions symbolically as they were for the last days; the days that you and I live in. So the description of these visions can be quite confusing to the untrained mind. Since my book is about the time of the end I will only cover the key prophecies of Revelation pertaining to our time.

Before we begin, keep in mind that in many end time prophecies duality comes into play, representing visions and prophecies that may apply to more than one nation, time in history, and meaning. For example when one reads of Babylon, it may refer to ancient Babylon or to Babylon of the last days. With careful study and cross referencing of scriptures, you can and will correctly interpret the prophecies. With that said let's move on to the phases of judgments during the apocalypse.

Rev. Chapter 6 and 7 - Jesus has a scroll in his hand with 7 seals. When He opens the seals of the scroll - each one announces the Judgments that are to come upon the whole earth. The first four scrolls reveal the four horsemen of the apocalypse. These are not literal men riding on horses but rather they are symbolic of the events that will be unfolding during the great tribulation (apocalypse). I believe these events will occur in rapid succession one after another; hence the vision of horses in motion; one immediately after the other.

The Seven Seal Judgments

The 1st Seal is the first horse - a white horse whose rider has a bow but no arrows. This may be describing **the Antichrist** (man of perdition) that is to come, masquerading as a savior with peaceful intentions, and thus conquering an unsuspecting world through deceptive means (**Rev. 6:2**).

The 2nd Seal is the second horse - a rider on a red horse carrying a great sword to take peace from the earth, **so that people could kill one another**. This is clearly symbolizing war among the nation - perhaps **World War III** (**Rev. 6:4**).

The 3rd Seal is the third horse - a rider on a black horse carrying scales on his hand and based on what is said in this passage, it is revealing **a great famine throughout the world**; a great shortage of food supplies as a result of devastated lands due to the war released by the second seal (**Rev. 5-6**)

The 4th Seal is the fourth horse - a rider on an ashen (grayish green) horse symbolizing death and hell. This rider is **symbolic of the beast kingdom consisting of the ten nation confederacy**. Notice that the rider is referring to "*them*" and not "*him*". It further states that "power was given to them over a fourth of the earth, to kill with sword, with hunger, with death, and the beasts of the earth." I believe this fourth rider is the final beast kingdom under control of the man of perdition that destroys 1/4th of the earth - possibly with weapons of mass destruction! I believe that the "**beasts of the earth**" is NOT referring to lions, bears and other predator animals but rather the leaders of the beast kingdom, consisting of the ten nation confederacy and the henchmen that martyr the saints as we read in the fifth seal that follows.

Note: The term "***beast***" refers to the beast kingdom and all the people that associate with it, and who worship the beast (Satan) and take his mark (the mark of the beast).

5th Seal - reveals a great persecution and Martyrdom of a myriad of saints by the beast kingdom because of their testimony/witness of the name of Jesus Christ as the son of God in accordance with the word of God, in the Holy bible. These who are referred to as "**saints**" are the Christians and elect who are beheaded or killed by other means because they do not bow down and worship the Antichrist (Satan's man of perdition), who has come to full power over the earth after the fourth seal above.

Important Note: The revelation clearly reveals that the saints (all Christians - the body of Christ) will be targeted and hated not just by the one world government but most of the inhabitants of the world who will be brainwashed into believing that the antichrist is God, and the false prophet is Jesus! That is why they will gladly take the mark of the beast. This hatred towards all witnesses of the Lord is clearly revealed in various places including **Rev. 11:10**, when the inhabitants of the earth celebrate when the two witnesses appointed by God to witness to the world in an effort to save as many souls as possible, are killed by the man of perdition (Satan's representative on earth).

6th Seal - A great Earthquake rocks the planet.

7th Seal - when the seventh seal is released, there is silence in Heaven for 1/2 hour, and seven angels are given seven trumpets in preparation of the release of the trumpet judgments of God. This appears to be a transition point, a short period of rest, perhaps to allow for some to repent before the trumpet judgments begin.

NOTE: This period of rest at the seventh seal is interesting when we consider that the Lord rested on the seventh day and sanctified it (made it Holy), and how he commands you and I to do the same. Obviously the Sabbath day was never abolished as it is symbolically observed even in heaven during the apocalypse, and it is one of the Ten Commandments (**Exodus 20:8-11**). This may be another main reason why the **seventh seal** does not release any judgments upon the earth! When you study Revelation carefully as I have, you will perceive the level of perfect precision on how even the last seven years of the age of man unfold. It is like a religious or holy ceremony in heaven commemorating the end of this imperfect age.

The first 6 seals of Revelation chapter six appear to be a synopsis of the key events that will occur during the great tribulation, which *will NOT begin* until the man of perdition is finally revealed.

Note that these seal judgments are not necessarily direct judgments from God, but rather judgments and curses that man has brought upon himself by placing their faith in man, instead of in God!

The Seven Trumpet Judgments

Now let's move on to the seven trumpet judgments:
The trumpet Judgments are sounded by seven Angels. These angels are charged with executing God's judgments; the "wrath of God judgments". We can infer from **Rev. 6:10-11** that these judgments come upon the earth in large part because of the blood of the saints (God's children, the body of Christ) that was shed because of their testimony of God's word:

1) The first angel sounded his trumpet - which destroys all green grass, and _a third_ of all trees. (**Rev. 8:7**). This would obviously lead to a global famine, and many millions would die of starvation.

So the **first trumpet** appears to be describing a thermonuclear attack that destroys a third of earth (Note that the western hemisphere is one third of the earth). _**A third of the trees**_ were burned up as well as all green grass. One can imagine the enormous loss of life and the magnitude of the pestilence and famine that would affect the entire earth when one third of all trees are vaporized and _**all green grass**_ (i.e. vegetation) is burned up.

2) The second angel sounds his trumpet and a great mountain falls on the sea and a third of the sea became blood. This is NOT a literal mountain or literal blood, but is John's way of describing perhaps **a large asteroid** or **nuclear missiles** that land in the ocean and contaminate one third of the ocean water. As a direct result, **_one third_** of all sea creatures perish, and one third of the ships at sea are destroyed. Most likely tsunamis will also wreak havoc on many coastal areas (**Rev. 8:8-9**).

3) When the third angel sounds his trumpet - a great star fell from heaven burning like a torch, and this one contaminates **one third** of the rivers and springs of water, many men perish from drinking this water. This one may be caused by nuclear weapons (or again asteroids), because the description "burning like a torch" is more descriptive of an intercontinental ballistic missile (ICBM), and it contaminates drinking water, causing many people die from drinking it. Perhaps they are not aware of the level of radiation in this water thinking that the contamination is not so widespread (**Rev. 8:10-11**).
So this star is most likely one or several nuclear missiles impacting a land mass with rivers and springs of water. We also read here that a third of the earth is darkened due to this nuclear attack on an area of the globe, resulting in great death.

4) The fourth angel sounded and "**_a third_** of the sun, moon, and stars were struck, so that a third of them were darkened and a third of the day did not shine (**Rev. 8:12**). This must mean that one third of the earth has been devastated either by a massive asteroid impact or thermo-nuclear exchange or related catastrophe.

Make note that so far **_one third_** of the earth's land mass is affected by the first four trumpet blasts? God is placing great emphasis on this, which leads me to believe that the great tribulation will begin when a large land and ocean area of the world is devastated.

In **Rev. 8:13** we are warned that the next 3 trumpet judgments are going to make things even worse for the remaining inhabitants of the earth.

Note: Given the **Rev. 8:13** warning, it is hard to imagine as I write this in early December 2014, how progressively bad things will actually get. This is **_probably because at this point the restrainer is removed_** from the earth giving Satan power to wreak maximum havoc over this planet.

We should all **_pray_** that God indeed will rapture His elect - the church (the body of Christ) before the great tribulation begins, as many theologians believe (Pre-tribulation rapture)! But when we read in the revelations that a myriad (millions) of saints will be martyred during the apocalypse, one must wonder and prepare for a mid or post rapture of the saints. Regardless, we must remain prepared and ready since our appointed time to meet our maker can be at any moment.

5) The fifth angel sounds his trumpet - A Star (perhaps a fallen angel) falls from heaven and has been given the key to the bottomless pit (Hades/hell). He opens the bottomless pit and smoke arose out of the pit like the smoke of a great furnace (**Rev. 9:1-2**). This may be describing a massive volcanic eruption which also shoots out smoke just like a great furnace!

The fifth trumpet also releases evil spirits from Hades who afflict all men except the 144,000 who have the seal of God on their forehead and who have been granted special protection from God (**Rev. 9:3-11**).

The locusts that arise out of the bottomless pit as a result of the fifth trumpet could be some form of **germ warfare** or **manufactured virus** since they do not harm the vegetation but only the inhabitants of the earth; specifically those who do not have the seal of God on their forehead (i.e. the 144,000). This germ or virus apparently affects the body for five months; perhaps a vaccine is developed to curtail the pandemic. Jesus does warn in **Mathew 24**, that the end of day judgments will include pestilence and disease (such as the Ebola virus outbreak of 2014).

Note: The revelation that demons are instructed to afflict only the non-believers, should be a reminder to all that Satan is NOT even a friend to the non-believers. Satan does not discriminate, he hates anything associated with God and equally, and is bent on destroying it all and taking it all to hell with him. This includes the grass, trees, planet earth and all human beings which were all created in the image of God.

6) The sixth angel sounds his trumpet - and four **_fallen_** Angels which were bound at the Euphrates River are released (**Rev. 9:14-15**). These evil angelic beings were so powerful that they had to be physically restrained until this moment in time.

The Euphrates River runs through Iraq. This may be indicating that the area of Iraq (where the terror army called ISIS is presently based), and the Middle East as a whole may be ground zero for the establishment of the beast kingdom and headquarters of the man of perdition. Also interesting how this area of the Middle East has always been an area of Jewish and Christian intolerance and persecution.
These four fallen angels kill a third of mankind, with a massive 200,000,000 man army which once the demonic influences are released in that region, invade from the east.

They are able to do this by influencing an army of 200 million; this may be a continuation or beginning of World War III that was announced at the opening of the aforementioned second and fourth seals.

Note: In John's time an army that size was impossible. Today it is quite possible considering the nearly seven billion worldwide population. We also discover that this army will kill one third of mankind with the use of weapons that rain down fire and brimstone **which again reads to me like nuclear weaponry (Rev. 9:15-18)**.

Rev. 9:20-21 makes it clear why these judgments continue to persist to the very end, as those who survive through all of the prior judgments still refuse to repent from worshipping demons, idols, sorcery, murder, sexual immorality and thefts.

The seventh angel sounds his trumpet and we have another break from the Judgments; **_another Sabbath break_** in between the trumpet and the final bowl judgments. Victory is proclaimed in heaven and a celebration commences as the angels and elders announce that the kingdoms of this world are now the kingdoms of the Lord; as the Messiah prepares for His triumphant second coming!

The Sabbath is to be a day where we stop all work and worship the Lord; thanking Him for the prior week's blessings. On this day we pray, nourish our spirit with the word, and develop our relationship with the Lord. We saw that after the sixth seal was released, Revelation chapter seven is an instructional chapter. Once again after the sixth trumpet judgment in Revelation chapter nine, chapter ten is also an instructional chapter right through Rev. 11 verse 14 when the seventh trumpet judgment is released.

After the seventh trumpet judgment, Revelation chapters 12 through 15 are instructional chapters as well which describe the following:

Rev. Ch. 12: This chapter covers the cosmic battle that Satan has waged against Israel, and mankind. Note that he is NO MATCH to Jesus and God, so that he can only attempt to defeat Jesus and God through mankind! ***Satan knows he already lost his battle against the Messiah almost 2,000 years ago when Jesus Christ became our sacrificial Lamb at the cross, allowing anyone who acknowledges and accepts His sacrifice the right to become children of the Most High***! Messiah has **already** earned the deed to planet earth and the universe. In His mercy He is just waiting for the full number of saved souls to be reached before He returns (**Rev. 6:10-11**)!

Rev. Ch. 13: This chapter describes the antichrist, false prophet and the beast kingdom that will reign approximately three and one half years before the second coming.

Rev. Ch. 14 and 15: are celebratory chapters in heaven whereby the angels and the saints (all those who were previously martyred because they refused the mark of Satan) prepare for the final series of judgments and the return of the Messiah to establish a new heaven and a new earth - one that is purified, and cleansed of all sin). Some scholars believe that by this point the rapture may have already occurred.

The Final Seven Bowl Judgments

Now we move on to the last series of judgments; the Bowl (also referred to as vial) judgments. Like the Trumpet judgments, the bowl judgments are also a part of the "**Wrath of God Judgments**". This series of judgments appears to be particularly for those who accepted the mark of Satan (mark of the beast), and all who refuse to repent.

1) The first Bowl is poured out and a horrible sore *afflicts all those who took the mark of the beast (Satan) and who worshiped his image*. I hope that you like I are finding it really hard to comprehend how so many will be so deceived by Satan in these last days into thinking that this coming demon possessed one world government leader of the final one world government is God or can actually defeat and or prevent the second coming of Messiah.

2) The second bowl is poured out on the sea and it became blood (contaminated). This time all the living creatures of the sea are dead (not just one third).

3) The third bowl is poured on all rivers and springs of water so that no drinkable water remains.

4) The fourth bowl is poured out and the sun scorches men with fire. Perhaps the ozone layer fails amidst all the level of contamination and radiation in the atmosphere.

5) The fifth bowl immerses the beast kingdom (the one world empire) in total darkness. I perceive that since with the fourth bowl there is a sun that scorches men with fire the sun now fries out the electrical grid (**Rev. 16:10-11**)

6) The sixth bowl dries up the Euphrates River which allows an army from the east (king of the East) the ability to cross over to engage in the **battle of Armageddon** along with other invading armies. This last battle is referred to as "**the great day of God Almighty**" (**Rev. 16:14**), probably because it brings an end to the age of man.

On or around the battle of Armageddon the Lord returns as we read in the verse that follows:

Rev. 16:15

"Behold, I am coming as a thief. Blessed is he who watches, and keeps his garments, lest he walks naked and they see his shame."

7 the seventh bowl judgment: After the seventh bowl judgment is poured out on the air a great voice declares ***"it is done"*** which releases the greatest earthquake in history. It must break the Richter scale along with everything else since the force of this quake collapses mountains and Islands.

This massive earthquake is the final event of the age of man as the remaining chapters of Revelation are instructional as follows:

Revelation 17 & 18: These are two very important prophecy chapters that describe who or what "**Babylon the Great**" is. This great entity is so important to end time events that God dedicates two full chapters to this topic. This will be covered in detail in another chapter.

Rev. 19: Describes the Messiah's second coming, with Jesus returning with His heavenly army to put an end to Satan and his minions. It also describes the Marriage Supper of the Lamb.

Rev. 20: Describes the Judgment of the antichrist, false prophet, Satan, the demons, zombies (sorry, I couldn't help it!), and all those who took the mark of the beast.

Rev. Chapter 21 - Describes the new Heavens and new earth - our glorious new home through eternity!

In Chapter 22: The revelation of Jesus Christ culminates in His words:
"I, Jesus, have sent my angel to give you this testimony for the churches. I am the Root and the Offspring of David, and the bright Morning Star."

To gain a more thorough understanding of the entire book of Revelation from beginning to end you may consider grabbing a copy of my new book: **"Revelation Mysteries Decoded"**

Chapter 8 - The Beast of Revelation of Chapters 13 & 17

This mystery is quite confusing if you are not familiar with ancient history. When John was writing this, about 95AD, there had been five great world powers; Egypt, Assyria, Babylon, Persia, and Greece. All had been conquered and absorbed. The current power was Rome, which was never really conquered and will re-emerge at the end of the age.

Who is the 666 - the Antichrist?

When I was writing the book "Revelation Mysteries Decoded", I was not sure how to address the mystery of the 666. While I wrote, I prayed for guidance. Then suddenly the spirit revealed to me what I needed to write about this mystery number. So in this section, I will share the larger message behind the 666.

When you look at the deteriorating shape of the world today, it doesn't take much to imagine conditions getting to a point where people will cry out for a leader who can bring order out of chaos. Whether the issue is climate change, the decline of the US dollar, the economic collapse of Europe or war in the Middle East, the one solution most leaders agree on is the need for some form of world government. With the things that already threaten world stability getting worse by the day, how much more frantic will people be after millions of their neighbors suddenly disappear in the rapture without warning or explanation, and there's been a war that brings destruction from Europe through the Middle East and into Russia? When people become convinced that their problems cannot be solved by human means alone they look to the supernatural for answers.

In the near future the world will experience a series of calamities, which could be from acts of God, and or man-made; such as a nuclear attack, a global economic meltdown, or some other crisis.

Then this charismatic person will emerge onto the world scene. The Antichrist (the beast) will persuade the inhabitants of the earth with his seductive charisma to embrace his solutions to the world's problems. He will seem to have solutions for just about everything including establishing peace throughout the world, and even uniting the nations, economies, and religions into what seems to be a cohesive and effective system. The world will worship this man.

The coming of the lawless one will be in accordance with the work of Satan displayed in all kinds of counterfeit miracles, signs and wonders, and in every sort of evil that deceives those who are perishing (**2 Thes. 2:9-10**)

A leader who promises to restore peace and safety and demonstrates miraculous power that astonishes everyone will soon emerge on the scene, and will quickly be given the reins of world government. By many accounts, this lawless one is standing in the wings as you read this, awaiting his cue.

The man of perdition will rule politically, economically, and religiously, speaking great blasphemies against God and setting himself up in the Temple as God himself. Yet he will be the very opposite of God. The Antichrist is called different things such as:

The Prince Who is to Come – Daniel 9:26 (NLT)
The Worthless Shepherd – Zechariah 11:17 (NLT))
The Man of Lawlessness – 2 Thessalonians 2:3 (NLT)
The One Who Brings Destruction – 2 Thessalonians 2:3 (NLT)
The Beast – Revelation 13:11 (NLT)

Many people have tried to identify this antichrist throughout time, and all have failed since he has not yet appeared on scene - or hasn't he? The book of Revelation refers to this person as the man of perdition, the beast and assigned the number "666" to him. He will be the leader of the beast kingdom, the last kingdom that reigns on earth before the second coming.

The 666 identifies the antichrist, but note that the number 6 is representative of the number of man. Man was created on the sixth day, so the number 666 may be referring to the totality of fallen man; those who take the mark of the beast during the apocalypse; the tribulation period of seven years (**Rev. 13:16**)! Once they take the mark they will be imparted with the spirit of antichrist and will in turn also become a beast, or a part of the beast - the **666**.

So the **666** is the absolute opposite of **777** which is the kingdom of God, which includes all the saints in their totality (the body of Christ)!

Those unrepentant lost souls, which are referred to as "***the inhabitants of the earth***" in the book of Revelation, are those that will support, empower and feed the beast and the beast kingdom by taking the mark of the beast. Once they take the mark, these are held equally guilty by enabling the antichrist and false prophet to gain the full power, influence and authority needed to control the earth at the time of the end! They are forbidden from ever entering God's kingdom because they have sold their soul to Satan. This is why their condemnation is equally fierce as we read in **Revelation 14:9-11**.

So many have been trying to unlock the mystery of **666**, and all this time the enemy may have been inside of every man who refuses to worship and obey the God of the universe! In the last days the **666** will most definitely apply to all, the many millions - perhaps billions who will side with and worship Satan by taking his mark - the "**mark of the beast**"!

Once they make that covenant with the devil these lost souls will become part of the beast and this is why it will be impossible for such inhabitants to ever repent or be forgiven. Once they take that mark, it is as if they instantly inherit the DNA of the devil - so that it will be inherently impossible for these individuals to repent, to feel remorse or retain their conscience.

In the time of the end, he will reveal his true nature and he will require the world to worship him as god. Incredibly most will do just that by willingly taking up his mark on their hand or forehead, referred to as the mark of the beast (**Revelation 13:16-17**). BTW, "the inhabitants of the earth" is the term used in Revelation for those void of the Holy Spirit in the last days - otherwise they would be referred to as man, people or mankind.

Revelation 13:16-17

"He causes all, both small and great, rich and poor, free and slave, to receive a mark on their right hand or on their foreheads, and that no one may buy or sell except one who has the mark or the name of the beast, or the number of his name."

What the Prophecies reveal about the Antichrist's Personality

Personality of the Antichrist: Throughout the Bible, we are granted insight into the personality and disposition of the Antichrist. We are told how he will act, what he will do, and where he will get his power. Although far from exhaustive, the Scriptures provide us with many clues.

Arrogance: The Antichrist will be arrogant: "This little horn had eyes like human eyes and _**a mouth that was boasting arrogantly**_."

Daniel 7:8 "The king will do as he pleases, exalting himself and claiming to be greater than every god there is, even blaspheming the God of gods."

Daniel 11:36 The Antichrist will be so filled with self-love and arrogance that he will launch a rebellion against God Almighty. He will place himself above all others, and even set himself up in the Jewish Temple, proclaiming to be God.
Satan's Power --- The Antichrist will be empowered by Satan: "He will become very strong, but not by his own power."

Daniel 8:24 "This evil man will come to do the work of Satan with counterfeit power and signs and miracles. He will use every kind of wicked deception to fool those who are on their way to destruction because they refuse to believe the truth that would save them." **2 Thessalonians 2:9-10**

"And the dragon gave him his own power and throne and great authority."
Revelation 13:2

The Bible clearly states that the Antichrist will derive his power from Satan. In fact, following the Devil's banishment from heaven (**Revelation 12:9**), he will indwell the Antichrist, making this man of lawlessness the literal embodiment of Satan.

Lust for Power - The Antichrist will be consumed with power, and power alone will he worship: "He will have no regard for the god of his ancestors, or for the god beloved of women, or for any other god, for he will boast that he is greater than them all. Instead of these, he will worship the god of fortresses; a god his ancestors never knew and lavish on him gold, silver, precious stones, and costly gifts." **Daniel 11:37-38**

"They worshiped the dragon for giving the beast such power, and they worshiped the beast. 'Is there anyone as great as the beast?' they exclaimed. 'Who is able to fight against him?'" **Revelation 13:4**

The Antichrist will only acknowledge one power, a military power he possesses. **His power will be so great, the people of the world will marvel in wonder and worship it**, asking the rhetorical question of who among them is able to fight against his mighty kingdom.

Antichrists arrival onto the World Scene

In addition to various aspects of his character, the Bible provides us with some details about the career of this man of lawlessness, beginning with his meteoric rise to fame from among ten kings.

He rises from among 10 Kings (nations):
"It was different from any of the other beasts, and it had ten horns. As I was looking at the horns,

suddenly another small horn appeared among them." **Daniel 7:7-8**

"His ten horns are ten kings who have not yet risen to power; they will be appointed to their **kingdoms** for one brief moment to reign with the beast. They will all agree to give their power and authority to him" **Revelation 17:12-13.**

The ten kings will surrender their power and national sovereignty to the beast kingdom. From among them, the Antichrist will be elected or appoint himself as supreme leader.

The man of perdition then subdues 3 of the 10 nations: "Three of the first horns were wrenched out, roots and all, to make room for it." **Daniel 7:8.**
Apparently, three of the ten nations will oppose the Antichrist and his brazen power grab. In the struggle that ensues, he will defeat them, and his control over the new world government will be absolute.

He makes a 7 year treaty with Israel: "He will make a treaty with the people for a period of seven years" **Daniel 9:27**.

The Antichrist will make a treaty with the people of Israel for a period of seven years.
The details and nature of this treaty are yet unknown. Based on prior failed treaties, Israel will agree to rely on this one world leader for its

security. Of course this final treaty will also be a false one.

Since America has been Israel's protector in the past, either America has turned its back on Israel or America is no longer capable of protecting Israel (read the chapter on Babylon the Great), opening the door for the one world leader to make such a treaty.

He Will Conquer Many: **Rev. Chapter 6** describes the Antichrist as a great conqueror riding on a white horse. He goes out to conquer many, and he wields a great sword. In his conquest, he will kill a sizeable portion of the world's population.

Antichrist Will Rule Politically, Religiously, and Economically

"He (False Prophet) exercised all the authority of the first beast. And he required all the earth and those who belong to this world to worship the first beast, who's death-wound had been healed."
Revelation 13:12
The False prophet (second beast) is the second in command after the antichrist and will exercise all the authority of the first beast. He will require the world to worship and give allegiance to the antichrist.
"And he was given authority to rule over every tribe and people and language and nation." **Revelation 13:7**

Not one person will escape the reach of the

Antichrist and his governmental dominion.
"He required everyone – great and small, rich and poor, slave and free – to be given a mark on the right hand or on the forehead. And no one could buy or sell anything without that mark, which was either the name of the beast or the number representing his name (**Revelation 13:16-17).**

The antichrist will have unprecedented control over the world's financial transactions. He will have so much power that he will be able to determine on a case-by-case basis which individuals will be allowed to buy or sell anything.

Unprecedented Destruction: In his insatiable quest for personal glory, the antichrist will cause great destruction.
"He will become very strong, but not by his own power. He will cause a shocking amount of destruction and succeed in everything he does."
Daniel 8:24

Abomination of Desolation Jesus prophesied of a time of great tribulation, such as the world had never seen, nor ever will see again. He said this time period will begin with the desecration of the Jewish Temple: "The time will come when you will see what Daniel the prophet spoke about: the sacrilegious object that causes desecration standing in the Holy Place." **Matthew 24:16 (NLT)**

In the middle of the tribulation period (which will also be the middle of the 7 year peace treaty with Israel) the antichrist will fulfill this prophesy by standing in the Jewish Temple and proclaiming to be God.

He will set up an image in the Holy Place and demand that the world worship it.
"He will put an end to the sacrifices and offerings. Then as a climax to all his terrible deeds, he will set up a sacrilegious object that causes desecration, until the end that has been decreed is poured out on this defiler." **Daniel 9:27**

"He will exalt himself and defy every god there is and tear down every object of adoration and worship. He will position himself in the temple of God, claiming that he himself is God." **2 Thessalonians 2:4**

He Destroys All Religions But His Own:

Rev. Chapter 13 reveals that once the antichrist arrives on the scene he will quickly appoint a false prophet who will establish a one world religion.
This religion at first will encompass several religions in an attempt to appease as many religious leaders as possible and to attract mass appeal. Then, once he has everybody sucked into this religious order, the antichrist (who by this point will be the one world leader) will proclaim that he is God, and he will require all to worship only him, and those who refuse will be martyred.

This is another reason why John in revelation attributes Roman characteristics to this end time beast kingdom, since during his time the Roman emperor required all to worship only him or they would be exiled (like John was) or put to death!

Then at the mid-point of the seven year tribulation period, he will claim that he is god and he requires all people to worship him and his image, and to put his mark on their forehead or hand.

He Wages War against the Saints:

Of course God's elect, those written in the "Book of Life" will refuse to take the mark of the beast. Thus the antichrist will commence a worldwide campaign to destroy all Christians, Jews and anyone else who refuses the mark.
"And the beast was allowed to wage war against God's holy people and overcome them."
Revelation 13:7

Kills Two-Thirds of the Jewish People: In his rage against the Jewish people, the Antichrist will manage to kill two-thirds of the Jewish race. "Two-thirds of the people in the land will be cut off and die, says the Lord. But a third will be left in the land." **Zechariah 13:8-9**

"He will destroy powerful leaders and devastate the holy people. He will be a master of deception, defeating many by catching them off guard. Without warning he will destroy them. He will even take on the Prince of princes in battle, but he will be broken, though not by human power" **Daniel 8:24-25.**

So Jesus Himself will be the only one who will succeed at destroying the antichrist upon His second coming.

He Wages War against Jesus Christ

In his blind arrogance, the Antichrist will lead a rebellion against Jesus Christ Himself!
"He will even take on the Prince of princes in battle." **Daniel 8:25**
 "And I saw three evil spirits that looked like frogs leap from the mouth of the dragon, the beast, and the false prophet. These miracle-working demons caused all the rulers of the world to *gather for battle against the Lord on that great judgment day of God Almighty*." **Revelation 16:13-14**
His Ultimate Destruction: Despite his worldly success, the reign of the Antichrist will be relatively brief, seven years max.

Battle of Armageddon:

While gathering the armies of the world to Jerusalem to wage battle against the Lord, the antichrist will set up his camp and gather his armies in a place called Armageddon, the modern day city of Megiddo, Israel. "He will halt between the glorious holy mountain and the sea and will pitch his royal tents there, but while he is there, his time will suddenly run out, and there will be no one to help him." **Daniel 11:45**

"And they gathered all the rulers and their armies

to a place called Armageddon in Hebrew."
Revelation 16:16

He will lose this battle and it will be God Himself
that destroys this army.
"Both the beast and his false prophet were thrown
alive into the lake of fire that burns with sulfur."
Revelation 19:20
"But then the court will pass judgment, and all his
power will be taken away and completely
destroyed" **Daniel 7:26.**

Lake of Fire: As a result of his defeat, the
Antichrist will be cast into the lake of fire, where he
will be tormented forever.
Then the Lord's kingdom will be established here on
earth.

Why would anyone choose to take the Mark of the Beast knowing the Consequences thereof?
It is hard for many of God's people, let alone even
those who are on the

Sidelines, to accept that in the last days the world
will be so demon
possessed that it will hate and reject the God of
their fathers and
fore-fathers (the God of heaven) and embrace the
god of hell.

They will reject everything that has to do with God;
including the bible, the true church, Jesus Christ,
the Holy Spirit, and God Himself.

Instead, they will embrace everything Satan and that is why John in Revelation who is observing this corrupted end time kingdom refers to it as a beast, and the inhabitants of the earth who worship the beast figuratively as beasts as well. This is exactly what the book of Revelation reveals. These will all be blotted out of the "Book of Life" (they are sentenced to eternal damnation), because they choose to worship Satan and curse the God of heaven (read **Revelation: 13:8, 16:9 and 16:11**).

Once a person rejects God, their soul is totally void of the Holy Spirit of God, but the law of physics requires that the vacuum must be filled. And it will be filled with the opposite spirit of God; the demonic spirit of Satan. This is why they will "blindly" worship and follow the prince of darkness, the false prophet and one world dictator of **Revelation 13**.

So why would anyone take the mark?

1) Many will believe Satan's lie because they lack the knowledge of the word and of the prophecies.
2) Many will do it out of fear of execution or martyrdom.
3) Those with a lukewarm Spirit will be easily swayed by others into taking the mark.
4) Those that place their trust on their government or the media will fall for all the lies. Certainly world governments nor the media will be citing the

prophecies, nor heeding the warnings from the word of God, since they are unfamiliar with either. 5) Many do not want to forego the things of this world. The many who embrace the coming False Prophet, Antichrist, and one world religion will be easy prey for the devil. Sadly everyone not written in the Lambs Book of Life will worship the beast; that is everyone not elected for salvation!

Revelation 13:8

*"**All who dwell on the earth will worship him**, **whose names have not been written in the Book of Life** of the Lamb slain from the foundation of the world."*

And many who do not believe or read the bible, will fail to heed the stern warning from God below on what will happen to ALL who take the mark of the beast.

Revelation 14:

"Then a third angel followed them, saying with a loud voice, "If anyone worships the beast and his image, and receives his mark on his forehead or on his hand, he himself shall also drink of the wine of the wrath of God, which is poured out full strength into the cup of His indignation. He shall be tormented with fire and brimstone in the presence of the holy angels and in the presence of the Lamb."

The sealing of the 144,000 Jews

This event will apparently occur at the beginning of the tribulation period. These are the First Fruits of the Resurrection. 12,000 from each of the 12 tribes of Israel will be sealed with the mark of God on their forehead, thus protecting them from harm. They will apparently be engaged in a massive revival in an effort to save as many souls back to God, before the end of the age.

In addition to being reassuring in that holy men will be present on earth during the tribulation period, it is also a confirmation that God never gave up on the Jews - unlike what replacement theology want us to think.

It is also a revelation that there must be completeness; a fullness of the number of Jews and gentiles, before the final trumpet and bowl judgments can proceed.

"I saw another angel ascending from the rising of the sun, having the seal of the living God, and he called with a loud voice to the four angels who had been given power to damage earth and sea, saying, **"Do not damage the earth or the sea or the trees, until we have marked the servants of our God with a seal on their foreheads**. *And I heard the number of those who were sealed,* **one hundred forty-four thousand**, *sealed out of every tribe of the people of Israel"* **Revelation 7:2-4**

Note: These 144,000 will be sealed on their forehead as a sign of being marked / reserved for God. Interesting how Satan will want to have as many people marked on their forehead as a sign that they are marked / reserved for Satan! This is why anyone who takes the mark of the beast has forfeited any chance at redemption and salvation.

Chapter 9 - Who is "Babylon the Great" of Revelation 17 & 18?

This chapter is an excerpt from my book **"Babylon the Great is Fallen, is Fallen"** with updates where applicable.

In the book of Revelation Babylon the great is referred to as that **"great city which reigns over the kings of the earth"** (**Rev. 17:18**). Keep this in mind as we discover who may be this great nation.

Mystery Babylon the great is NOT ancient Babylon, as ancient Babylon does not fit most if any of the identifiers given in **Revelation 17 and 18**. If it was ancient Babylon as some theologians and others who shy away from end time prophecies profess, then it would not be referred to as a **"mystery"**! The term "mystery" is used by John in Revelation because the identity of this great nation was not revealed to John since this nation still did not exist at the time that John penned the book of Revelation.

Ancient Babylon was located in the plain of Shinar about 50 miles south of Baghdad. The capital city of ancient Babylon still lies in ruins today, and even though Saddam Hussein had tried to restore the ruins, he was ousted and executed before he could complete that task. Perhaps the hand of God was at work here preserving the prophecies that ensure that there remains a clear distinction between **old**

Babylon and **Babylon the great** at the time of the end. The prophecies have assured us that **_ancient_** or old Babylon would never be rebuilt.

So understand that "**Babylon the great**" (also referred to as mystery Babylon, and daughter of Babylon) is symbolic of a "great' nation that will reign during the time of the end.

The term Babylon is also symbolic of spiritual iniquity, specifically to describe a nation, or kingdom that becomes **arrogant and proud**. The term is derived from the Hebrew "**balal**", which means to "confound". We read about this in **Genesis 11:4-9** when Nimrod built a tower in an arrogant attempt to reach the heavens and to war with God! So **God collapsed the tower** and scattered the people throughout the world, confounding them with different languages so that they could no longer conspire as a united force to build the city in defiance of the Lords will.

Important note: The **Genesis 11:4-9** scenario comes to play once again in the last days when mankind, again under the spell of Satan, will attempt to unite its Governments, land, religion and economic system in an effort to have a world totally void of God's laws, and sovereignty. Just like Nimrod of Babel, the end time Babylon system will once again arrogantly attempt to unite in an effort to fight God Himself (**Revelation 13, Rev. 19:19**). We hear of this ongoing quest when leaders of nations repeatedly use phrases such as "**a new world order, "citizens of the world**" etc.

Who is Babylon the Great

Many people ask why there is so much reference in the prophecies of the bible regarding Babylon, Rome and Israel and not **America**, which is still the undisputed global economic, political, and military power. To that question I say, let's keep reading!

So let me share with you what the bible reveals about "***Babylon the great***":

1) **Babylon the great** is just as the term suggests ***"a great nation"***. Many bible scholars believe that the term refers to the totality of the nations that reign on earth just before the Lord's return (as many bible scholars believe). In a sense that may be the case since all nations will share in her judgment, but clearly the passages on this term refer also specifically to one nation, the "head of nations" (**Revelation 18:10**).

2) This nation will be totally destroyed in just ***one hour*** (**Rev. 18:10; 17; 19**)!

3) According to **Rev. 18:6; 8; 9; 10; 18; 21-23** she will be utterly destroyed as a result of a **surprise *attack*** - which **renders her defenseless**!

4) Babylon the great is a nation with a very large **Christian population**. (**Rev. 18:4**) She was **founded on Godly and bible principles**, but she loses her way with God before her destruction (**Rev. 18:14**).

5) She is the **greatest importer** of all kinds of goods throughout the world so that she has made other nations that sell their goods to her - very wealthy (**Rev. 18:3; 11**).

6) She is a very **arrogant nation** - considering herself indestructible (**Rev. 18:7**).

7) She was instrumental in the **development of nuclear weapons**, was the first nation to perfect and use nuclear bombs, as she is to receive a double dose back (**Rev. 18:6**).

8) Her destruction will be enormously felt throughout the world, and all the nations will be financially ruined as a result (**Rev. 18:9**).

9) This nation is the **richest nation on earth** (hence the golden cup reference), and the **most powerful** and **influential** nation at the time of her destruction (**Rev. 18:9; 16; Jeremiah 51:7**).

10) The merchants (supply ships; trade partners), and all who trade with her, observe her destruction at a great distance for fear of her torment (**nuclear fallout)** - and there is nothing they can do for her. God clearly wants our attention to this as it appears in more than one verse (**Rev. 18:10; 15; 17; Jeremiah 50:13; 51:8-9**).

11) She is a nation **surrounded by waters and has a global reach** since most of her imports arrive by sea, and her navy guards the oceans of the world. (**Rev.18:17**). Also we read in the

following verse:

"O you who dwell by many waters, abundant in treasures, your end has come..." **Jeremiah 51:13**

12) She is the **greatest importer of goods** in the world; an importer of all types of goods (**Rev. 18:12-13**).

13) At the time of her destruction, she will be **heavily indebted**, with a massive debt burden. In fact she seems to be undergoing internal strife in various areas (**Jeremiah 50:37**).

14) The destruction of this great nation, will consequently ***destroy the world economy***, and will lead to a ***massive shortage of food*** and ***drinkable water***, most probably due to the after effects of **nuclear fallout**.

15) Although the Judgment is from God by removing His veil of protection, Babylon ***will be destroyed by another nation*** or ***group of nations.*** God usually uses mankind to exact His justice (**Rev.17:16**), because in the Garden of Eden God gave man dominion over the earth.

16) This nation may enter into an unholy pact with the antichrist and false prophet because she may engage in persecution of Christians just before her end (**Rev. 18:20; 24**).

17) She may initially make a pact or treaty with the nation or group of nations that eventually betray

her - and this is why she appears to be caught by surprise. We read in **Jeremiah 50:43** how the leader of Babylon is in shock over the report of the destruction of his or her nation (surprise attack).

18) The nation(s) that destroys her will come from the **north** (such as Russia, and or the consortium of ten nations). Whichever nation destroys her, it is referred to as the "**king of the North**" empire as prophesied in the book of Daniel, and in Jeremiah as follows:

Jeremiah 50:3
"For out of the north a nation comes up against her, which shall make her land desolate, and no one shall dwell therein."

By now you should have a good idea of who Babylon the great is. If you don't know yet, no problem - just keep on reading. There is a lot more to uncover in this chapter.

Below is Revelation 18 in its entirety and I highlight the areas that support the above commentary:

Revelation 18 (NKJV)

1 "After these things I saw another angel coming down from heaven, having great authority and the earth was illuminated with his glory.
2 And he cried mightily with a loud voice, saying, "Babylon the great is fallen, is fallen, and has become a dwelling place of demons, a prison for

every foul spirit, and a cage for every unclean and hated bird!

3 for all the nations have drunk of the wine of the wrath of her fornication, the kings of the earth have committed fornication with her, and **the merchants of the earth have become rich through the abundance of her luxury.**"

4 And I heard another voice from heaven saying, **"Come out of her, my people,** lest you share in her sins, and lest you receive of her plagues.

5 For her sins have reached to heaven and God has remembered her iniquities.

6 Render to her just as she rendered to you, and **repay her double according to her works; in the cup which she has mixed, mix double for her.**

7 In the measure that **she glorified herself and lived luxuriously,** in the same measure give her torment and sorrow; for she says in her heart, **'I sit as queen, and am no widow, and will not see sorrow.'**

8 Therefore her plagues will come in one day— death and mourning and famine. And she will be **utterly burned with fire,** for strong is the Lord God who judges her.

9 "The kings of the earth who committed fornication and lived luxuriously with her will weep and lament for her, when they see the smoke of her burning,

10 standing at a distance for fear of her torment, saying, 'Alas, alas, that great city Babylon, that mighty city! For in **one hour** your judgment has come.'

11 "And the merchants of the earth will weep and mourn over her, for no one buys their merchandise anymore:
12 merchandise of gold and silver, precious stones and pearls, fine linen and purple, silk and scarlet, every kind of citron wood, every kind of object of ivory, every kind of object of most precious wood, bronze, iron, and marble;
13 and cinnamon and incense, fragrant oil and frankincense, wine and oil, fine flour and wheat, cattle and sheep, horses and chariots, **and bodies and souls of men.**
14 The fruit that your soul longed for has gone from you, and all the things which are rich and splendid have gone from you, and you shall find them no more at all.
15 The merchants of these things, who became rich by her, **will stand at a distance for fear of her torment,** weeping and wailing,
16 and saying, 'Alas, alas, that great city that was clothed in fine linen, purple, and scarlet, and adorned with gold and precious stones and pearls!
17 For in **one hour** such great riches came to nothing.' Every shipmaster, all who travel by ship, sailors, and as many as trade on the sea, **stood at a distance.**
18 and cried out when they saw the **smoke of her burning,** saying, 'What is like this great city?'
19 "They threw dust on their heads and cried out, weeping and wailing, and saying, 'Alas, alas, that great city, in which **all who had ships on the sea became rich by her wealth!** For in **one hour she** is made desolate.'

20 *"Rejoice over her, O heaven and you* **holy apostles and prophets***, for* **God has avenged you on her!"**

21 *Then a mighty angel took up a stone like a great millstone and threw it into the sea, saying, "Thus with violence the great city Babylon shall be thrown down, and shall not be found anymore.*

22 *The sound of harpists, musicians, flutists, and trumpeters shall not be heard in you anymore. No craftsman of any craft shall be found in you anymore, and the sound of a millstone shall not be heard in you anymore.*

23 *The light of a lamp shall not shine in you anymore, and the voice of bridegroom and bride shall not be heard in you anymore. For your merchants were the great men of the earth, for by your sorcery all the nations were deceived.*

24 And in her was found the blood of prophets and saints, and of all who were slain on the earth."

The Woman riding the Beast in Revelation 17

I believe that the woman riding the beast in Revelation 17 (referred to as a harlot or whore) **has dual representation**, like many other prophecies in the bible. In this case it may refer to the one world harlot religion and Babylon the Great. I will explain.

The Harlot Religion

The woman riding the beast may be representative of the coming one world religious system; which like many bible scholars, I believe may contain some Judeo-Christian rituals and principals. This religion is referred to as a **harlot religion** because it incorporates and mixes doctrines from other religions and mythology; hence the "harlot" and "whore" description. Just like a harlot sleeps around with many men, the false harlot religion of the last days mixes itself with many other religions, idols and false gods.

I believe this is why almost the entire world (except God's elect) will embrace the coming one world religion. And we are currently witnessing a global movement from various religious organizations (including the Vatican) to unite all religions.

The Babylon the Great Connection

I also believe she dually refers to **Babylon the great**. Let me prove my point with just one of the key passages:
As revealed in the prophecy, the beast kingdom which consists of ten nations, ***they hate Babylon the great. Revelation 17:16 reveals that later on when her guard is down - the 10 nations of the beast kingdom will launch a massive surprise attack to destroy Babylon!***

Let's continue with the rest of the identifiers:

1) The woman riding the beast sits on **many waters**; meaning a nation **surrounded by oceans and a nation that commands the world's seas - the USA** is surrounded by the great oceans and

it's navy patrols the seas of all seven continents (**Rev. 17:1**)!

2) This woman is also described as **very wealthy** (Rev. 17:5).

3) The description of the woman sitting on the beast indicates that *at first Babylon the great will be aligned* with the beast kingdom through some kind of union or pact. **She may even dominate it, as the head of the beast kingdom**, at least for a while (**Dan. 7:23-24; Revelation 17:3**).

4) On her forehead is written "Mystery, **Babylon the Great**...." This is the same name given to the great nation that reigns in the last days just before her destruction (**Rev. 17:5**).

5) Perhaps Babylon the great, at least initially embraces and perhaps enforces the one world religion which God refers to as blasphemy and an abomination (**Rev. 17:3-6**)

6) Babylon may also enforce the worship of the beast (**Rev. 17:6**)

7) We know that the beast kingdom of Revelation 17 is under the influence and control of Satan since it ascends out of the bottomless pit, as the angel reveals. (**Rev. 17:8**)

8) The "**seven heads are seven mountains**" may refer to Rome (the city of seven hills), and also to

Babylon the great (**Hint:** America also has seven major mountain ranges). (**Rev. 17:9**)

9) **Revelation 17:11** speaks of the beast being an eighth king springing out of the seven heads. Just want to share that what this is saying is that the beast (Satan) becomes part of the beast kingdom since the coming beast kingdom is controlled, thinks like, and carries out the work of the devil.

10) The ten horns of the beast are 10 nations that are part of the beast kingdom (**Rev. 17:12**).

11) The woman also has global influence like Babylon the great does. (**Revelation 17:15**)

12) The ten nations (10 horns of the beast), will be under the authority of the beast kingdom, and they will be primarily charged with worldwide persecution and martyrdom of God's people. (**Rev 17:12-14**)

13) Just like all dictators and leaders controlled by Satan throughout history (like Hitler was), the beast's primary goal is to **glorify himself** and he will execute anyone who does not **worship him**. As we read in (**Rev. 13:15-17**) he will expend most of his energy to destroy God's people, His land, and if he could God himself. The latter being a battle that he cannot and will not win - although he will succeed in deceiving many millions into believing that Satan is god! He and his beast kingdom will literally die trying to usurp God and His plan of redemption (**Rev. 17:14, Rev. Chapters 19, and 20**).

14) Sadly we read in (**Rev. 13:8**) that the entire world will worship Satan, with the exception of God's elect (those written in the book of Life)

15) The **beast kingdom** (which will consist of a consortium of 10 nations) probably makes a pact with Babylon the great at the beginning of the Tribulation period, most likely to have her drop her guard. (**Revelation 17:16**)

16) As revealed in the prophecy, ***they hate this great nation (Babylon the great), and later on when her guard is down - the 10 nations of the beast kingdom will launch a massive surprise attack to destroy Babylon*** (**Revelation 17:16**).

17) Chapter 17 ends with the identification of the women, as the "**great city that reigns over the kings of the earth**", which as we already know is "**Babylon the great**"!

Below is Revelation chapter 17 with highlighted areas supporting the aforementioned:

Revelation 17

1 "*Then one of the seven angels who had the seven bowls came and talked with me, saying to me, "Come, I will show you the judgment of the* **great harlot who sits on many waters,** *2* **with** *whom the kings of the earth committed* fornication, and the inhabitants of the earth were made drunk with the wine of her fornication."

3 So he carried me away in the Spirit into the wilderness. And I saw a woman sitting on a scarlet beast which was full of names of blasphemy, having seven heads and ten horns.
4 The woman was arrayed in purple and scarlet, and adorned with gold and precious stones and pearls, having in her hand a golden **cup full of abominations** and the filthiness of her fornication
5 and on her forehead a name was written:

MYSTERY, **BABYLON THE GREAT,**
THE MOTHER OF HARLOTS
AND OF THE **ABOMINATIONS**
OF THE EARTH.

6 I saw the woman, drunk with the **blood of the saints** and with the blood of the martyrs of Jesus. And when I saw her, I marveled with great amazement.

7 but the angel said to me, "Why did you marvel? I will tell you the mystery of the woman and of the beast that carries her, which has the seven heads and the ten horns.
8 The beast that you saw was, and is not, and will ascend **out of the bottomless pit** and go to perdition. And those who dwell on the earth will marvel, whose names are not written in the Book of Life from the foundation of the world, when they see the beast that was, and is not, and yet is
9 "Here is the mind which has wisdom: The **seven heads are seven mountains** on which the woman

sits.

10 There are also seven kings. Five have fallen, one is, and the other has not yet come. And when he comes, he must continue a short time.

11 The beast that was, and is not, is himself also the eighth, and is of the seven, and is going to perdition.

12 "The **ten horns** *which you saw* **are ten kings** *who have received no kingdom as yet, but they receive* **authority for one hour as kings with the beast.**

13 These are of one mind, and they will give their power and authority to the beast.

14 These will make war with the Lamb, and the Lamb will overcome them, for He is Lord of lords and King of kings; and those who are with Him are called, chosen, and faithful."

15 Then he said to me, "The waters which you saw, where the harlot sits, are peoples, multitudes, nations, and tongues.

16 And the ten horns which you saw on the beast, these will hate the harlot, make her desolate and naked, eat her flesh and burn her with fire.

17 for God has put it into their hearts to fulfill His purpose, to be of one mind, and to give their kingdom to the beast, until the words of God are fulfilled.

18 And the **woman** *whom you saw is that* **great city** *which reigns over the kings of the Earth."*

Where is America in Bible Prophecy?

133

I believe that upon studying all of the passages I have shared with you so far that you will reach the same conclusion that I and other prophecy scholars have concluded - **Babylon the Great is America**!

So to those who ask "where is America in the end of day prophecies", I respond that **I see America in many places in the prophecies** of the bible.

As of December, 2014 **America is still the most powerful nation in the world** and **the leader of the free world**. Common sense dictates that the USA is therefore that "**Great City**" referred to in **Revelation 18**. America has certainly been greatly blessed because of the core values that it once held. _But a nation can lose its prowess rather quickly, especially when a superpower becomes arrogant and mocks God through liberal and unrighteous laws (iniquity)._ In the book of Daniel we learn how ancient Babylon was invaded and taken over by Media Persia in just one evening!

In Genesis we also read how Sodom and Gomorrah (**Genesis 19:24**) was destroyed with fire and brimstone in just one night, just like _**Babylon the Great**_ will be destroyed in one hour (also by fire) as we read in **Revelation 18**.

So since America did not exist during the time that the prophecies were penned, it takes some effort to unlock prophecies related to the USA, but as you have read, it just takes eyes and ears that a open to the truth. Let's go over some key passages:

Revelation 18:9-10

*"The kings of the earth who committed fornication and lived **luxuriously** with her will weep and lament for her, when they see the **smoke of her burning**, **standing at a distance for fear of her torment**, saying, 'Alas, alas, that **great city** Babylon, that mighty city! **For in one hour** your judgment has come.'*

Revelation 18:11

*11 "And the merchants of the earth will weep and mourn over her, for no one **buys** their merchandise anymore"*

Revelation 18:15-19

15 "The merchants of these things, who became rich by her, will stand at a distance for fear of her torment, weeping and wailing,
*16 and saying, '**Alas, alas, that great city that was clothed in fine linen, purple, and scarlet, and adorned with gold and precious stones and pearls!***
*17 For in **one hour such great riches** came to nothing.' Every shipmaster, all who travel by ship, sailors, and as many as trade on the sea, stood at a distance*
18 and cried out when they saw the smoke of her burning, saying, 'What is like this great city?'
*19 They threw dust on their heads and cried out, weeping and wailing, and saying, '**Alas, alas, that great city, in which all that had ships on the sea became rich by her wealth!** For **in one hour** she is made desolate."*

Obviously the "**great city**" term used in **Rev. 18:19** is referring to a "**great nation**", since no city can make many merchants (nations) throughout the world rich!

Did you catch what **Revelation 18:10** is revealing? Let's read:

"standing at a distance for fear of her torment, saying, 'Alas, alas, that great city Babylon, that mighty city! For in one hour your judgment has come".

This passage makes it abundantly clear that Babylon the great will most likely be **destroyed in one hour** by means of a massive **nuclear missile attack**; and these merchants are observing at a distance for fear of the **nuclear fallout**! No dirty bombs are going to inflict such final destruction on this **mighty** nation.

Anyone who thinks that a nuclear holocaust is a thing of the past clearly is not in touch with reality. The nuclear threat which began in the 1950's persists today, and even at a much greater scale since now even several rogue nations who HATE America also possess nuclear weapons.

When the Twin Towers fell on 9/11 they collapsed in the space of an hour or so. Was this a wake-up call; a harbinger of something much bigger to come?

Nobody wants to talk about the unspeakable anymore. The doomsday clock has been moth balled, and moved away from the public eye, but if it was still monitored, it would have been stuck at 12 midnight for quite a while!

To not want to hear about this grim reality is one thing, but to live in denial about it, or to consider it as mere fiction, will only keep us spiritually and emotionally unprepared.

In summary, with all unprejudiced honesty, consider what nation today December, 2014 fits the following passages to the letter...

1) "What nation that exists today do you think perfectly fits the description in **Revelation 18:15-19** above?
2) Which is the wealthiest nation on earth today?
3) Which is the most powerful nation on earth today?
4) Which is the most influential nation on earth today?
5) Which nation is the greatest importer of all types of goods in the world today, which has made many nations and merchants rich, throughout the earth?
6) Which nation has been referred to, even by its own leaders as "the greatest nation on earth (or as the bible coins it: "The Head of Nations")?

Indeed, **the USA** does fit the description of "**Babylon the Great**". It could certainly be destroyed in one hour through some kind of asteroid hit, nuclear attack, or through some other act of man or God - ***but as discussed in the prior chapter, the passages in Revelation 18 seem to strongly suggest a nuclear event that will lead to the massive food and drinkable water***

shortages prophesied in Revelation 8:7, and Rev. 16:3-4.

In just one event during the apocalypse, one third of the earth is prophesied to be destroyed. The prophecies imply that it is the western hemisphere that gets hit first, since the "***king of the west***" is not one of the nations mentioned during the great tribulation in neither the books of Daniel or Revelation. Also, God remembers Babylon the Great in **Revelation 16:19** implying that she is no longer around for the final bowl judgment.

Of course if the Western hemisphere is destroyed, it will pretty much devastate the entire world. A worldwide famine and economic collapse is certain to immediately follow such a colossal catastrophe. The Satan possessed nations that initiate the nuclear attack would have a terroristic mindset, willing to sacrifice themselves to achieve their evil objectives!

Notwithstanding, God is not limited on how He controls or alters the destiny of mankind and nations. God is not restricted by the laws of nature, physics or man.

America has been **greatly blessed** and more than any other nation in the past 200 years because it was founded with strong Judeo-Christian values and it has always been the defender of Israel. Perhaps God appointed America for this period of time as Israel's big brother and it has surely played that role since the miraculous re-formation of Israel as a state in 1948. But as already noted in the past decade or so, the USA has gradually wanted to separate itself from that **"big brother"** role, perhaps intimidated by 9-11, or perhaps because its influence in the Mid-East region has been mitigated somewhat as the nations of **Ezekiel 38** gain more control and influence in that region - in these last days.

Chapter 10 - The Book of Jeremiah and the Apocalypse

Jeremiah Ch. 50 and 51 are chapters on Babylon the Great, a symbolic name for the great nation that reigns in the last days, before she is destroyed by the beast nation. These passages all compliment the passages in **Revelation Ch. 17 and 18**; with identical and additional describing characteristics of the Babylon that reigns during the apocalypse!

Below are some passages that further identify America as Babylon the great. Note that I have added comments after each passage where appropriate.

Jeremiah 50 References to Babylon the Great

Jer. 50:8 - Here we are again warned to **escape** before her judgment.

Jer. 50:9 - An assembly of great nations **from the north** will attack Babylon with precision weapons (i.e. Guided missiles/ICBMs).

Jer. 50:12 - "*Your **mother** shall be deeply ashamed; she who bore you shall be ashamed*". America unlike Ancient Babylon was birthed from another nation (Britain).

Jer. 50:13 - "*...Everyone who goes by Babylon shall be horrified and hiss at all her plagues.*" This verse confirms what Revelation states; that she will be utterly destroyed.

Jer. 50:14 - *"...shoot at her, spare no arrows"*. This indicates that it will not be just a few missiles lobbed at Babylon, but a massive attack, which explains the multiple prophecies that she will be utterly destroyed.

Jer. 50:23 - *"How the **hammer of the whole earth** has been cut apart and broken! How Babylon has become a desolation among the nations!"* America's military might can be likened to the hammer of the whole earth.

Jer. 50:24 - *"I have laid a snare for you; You have indeed been trapped, O Babylon, And you were not aware;"* As I have contended throughout, Babylon the Great will be destroyed by a **surprise attack** - kind of like 9/11 caught her by **total** surprise."

Jer. 50:25 - *"The Lord has opened His armory, and has brought out the weapons of His indignation"*. This implies that very sophisticated weapons of mass destruction will be used to destroy Babylon the great.

Jer. 50:26 - She will be **utterly destroyed**.

Jer. 50:29a - "Call together the archers against Babylon. All you who bend the bow encamp against it all around;" Arrows are being symbolically used here since **ICBMs (guided nuclear missiles)** did not exist in Jeremiah's time.

Jer. 50:29b - "According to all she has done, do to her". This appears to be another hint to nuclear weaponry being used against her since America developed **nuclear weaponry** and was the first nation to ever use them.

Jer. 50:31 - "Behold, I am against you, o most **haughty** one!" says the Lord God of hosts". This means that she is a **very arrogant** nation.

Jer. 50:32 - "I will kindle a **fire in her cities**, and it will devour all around her." This passage again confirms that she will be **consumed by fire**.

Jer. 50:37 - She is a nation of mingled/mixed people; meaning a nation of immigrants; a perfect description of America.

Jer. 50:38 - "A drought is against her waters, and they will be dried up." As of this writing America is experiencing a massive drought in California.

Jer. 50:43 - *The king of Babylon has heard the report about them, and his hands grow feeble".* This passage is another indication that she will be **caught by surprise** when her destruction comes.

Now let's move on to Jeremiah 51

Jer. 51:6 - We read another plea from God for His people to flee Babylon. Remember that America houses the greatest population of Jews; even more than in Israel itself! No wonder we were so blessed. But here God is admonishing His people to get out of Babylon, because the blessings are replaced with judgment.

Jer. 51:6; 51:45; 51:50 - "Flee from the midst of Babylon," God does not waste words so He is emphasizing to those living in Babylon how bad it will be. In **Jer. 51:50** we have a clue that God is speaking to the Jews in Babylon when He instructs them to escape to Jerusalem, and again, America hosts the largest population of Jews in the world.

Jer. 51:7 - "Babylon was a *golden cup* in the Lord's hand," America evangelized the world sending ministers to all parts of the earth, and she is also the richest nation per capita. We were blessed accordingly. But today she has lost her ways.

Isaiah Chapter 5:1-7 and Mathew 21:33 - talks about the same Vineyard - Jesus puts himself into the prophecy saying that he is the one rejected by the Jews and so that is why Israel would be destroyed (AD 70) - and the Kingdom of God would be taken away from them and given to a ***NATION Bearing the fruits of it* - it being the Lord of the Vineyard - Jesus Christ**! America has spread the bible throughout the world. England also did that in their empire days. This is NOT replacement theology - instead it is saying that America has been given the task to preach the gospel throughout the world - for a season. **We became the Priests to the nations that Israel was to be**!

Jer. 51:8 - *"Babylon has suddenly fallen and been destroyed. Wail for her! Take balm for her pain; perhaps she may be healed. We would have healed Babylon, but she is not healed. **Forsake her**, and let us go everyone to his own country; **for her judgment reaches to heaven and is lifted up to the skies**."*

The nations that were trading partners with her desire to assist her, but they quickly give up on any attempt to aid Babylon because her destruction is irreparable and final. In Revelation we also discover that she is burned with fire and destroyed in one hour and that her torment reaches the heavens - all clear signs that nuclear weaponry and resultant radiation contamination makes any attempts at rescue impossible.

Jer. 51:11; 51:28 - *"Make the arrows bright! Gather the shields! The Lord has raised up the **spirit of the kings of the Medes**. For His plan is against Babylon to destroy it, because it is the vengeance of the Lord, the vengeance for His temple."*

NOTE: With the phrase "Make the arrows bright", one can picture a missile with its bright flame soaring through the sky. The Kings of the Medes will destroy Babylon the great. Some believe the kings of the Medes are Russia, but ancient maps identify it as Iran. Now it may include Russia as part of a coalition of ten nations (as prophesied elsewhere), but note that the "**kings**" of the Medes is plural and refers to more than one nation.

"Medes" refers to the areas of **Iran, Turkey, Iraq, and perhaps surrounding nations** (Iraq is the area that ISIS is currently trying to unite)! Again, the Medes are most related to modern day Iran - the nation developing Nuclear weapons and technology!

Jer. 51:13 - *"O you who dwell by **many waters, abundant in treasures**, your end has come"*

No doubt America has abundant treasures and dwells in many waters both physically and military. Our nation is surrounded by oceans, and our Navy patrols the seas of the world.

Jer. 51:33 - *"For thus says the Lord of hosts, the God of Israel: "The daughter of Babylon is like a threshing floor when it is time to thresh her; Yet a little while and the time of her **harvest will come**."* The harvest here refers to the rapture. So I believe that this passage reveals that **Babylon the Great will be destroyed before the rapture;** apparently everyone including God's elect will be here when she is destroyed!

Jer. 51:49; Rev. 18:24 - *"As Babylon has caused the slain of Israel to fall, so at Babylon the slain of all the earth shall fall."*

Apparently the USA may abandon Israel in the last days when she is invaded, and thus she is held guilty for all the slain of the earth as a result - hence the magnitude of her judgment.

Jer. 51:53 - *"Though Babylon were to mount up to heaven, and though she were to fortify the height of her strength, yet **from Me plunderers would come to her**," says the Lord.*

The USA was the first nation to land a man on the moon, and recently scrapped the manned space program. Also at one time the Twin Towers at the World Trade Centers were the tallest towers in the world, until on 9/11/2001 when plunderers in the form of terrorists collapsed both towers. In the space of one hour from impact, the towers fell!

Below are some other passages that describe America as Babylon the great:

Daughter of Babylon will be a nation of great wealth, these verses further address the issue of great national wealth:

1) "... because ye are grown fat as the heifer at grass..." (**Jeremiah 50: 12)**

2) "... a sword is upon her treasures..." (**Jeremiah 50: 37**)

3) "You who... are rich in treasures..." (**Jeremiah 51: 13)**

4) "The woman was dressed in purple and scarlet, and was glittering with gold, precious stones and pearls" (**Revelation 17: 4**).

5) "Give her as much torture and grief as the glory and luxury she gave herself" (**Revelation 18: 7**)

6) "When the kings of the earth who committed adultery with her and shared her luxury..." (**Revelation 18: 9**)

7) "Woe! Woe, O great city, dressed in fine linen, purple and scarlet, and glittering with gold, precious stones and pearls! In one hour such great wealth has been brought to ruin!" (**Revelation 18: 16**)

8) America is the melting pot of the world (**Jer. 50:37**).

9) We are surrounded by many waters, with deep water ports that further identify us as the Babylon of **Rev. 18 and Jeremiah 51:13**

10) Jeremiah 51:53 identifies Babylon as a nation that mounts up to the heavens, but spoilers bring her down. On 9/11/2001 spoilers in the form of terrorists brought down the Twin Towers at the World Trade Center. We were also the first nation to land a man on the moon - but recently American ended the manned space program!

11) America is a land full of idols (**Jer. 50:38b; Rev. 18:22**). Many Americans worship its idols of the rich and famous actors, athletes and celebrities. We spread our idols throughout the world through our powerful media, Hollywood, and associated entertainment networks (referred to as sorceries). **Since we are all made in God's image it is easy for fallen man to worship** mere men, albeit those with charisma or superior earthly gifts, elevating them to heights that should only be

reserved to the sovereign God.
Hollywood is the entertainment capitol of the world. Like the Magic world of Disney there is an Idol-like enchantment when we think of **Hollywood** and all the **"legendary" idols;** I mean actors, past and present.

12) We are the center of world commerce. One can surmise that New York City is the financial capital of the world **(Rev. 18:11-13).**

13) America has a large Jewish population; in fact the largest in the world, this may be why God warns His people to escape from Babylon to avoid sharing in her sins and her plagues **(Jeremiah 50:4-5; Rev. 18:4; Zech. 2:7; Isaiah 48:20; Jer. 50:5).**

14) The Kings of the Medes will destroy her (Jer. 51:11)...Some believe this means Russia, it may include Russia as part of a coalition but the kings of the Medes is plural and refers to more than one nation. Medes actually refers to the areas of Iran, Turkey, Iraq, and perhaps surrounding nations (Iraq is the area that ISIS is currently trying to unite)! The Medes are most related to modern day Iran - the nation developing Nuclear weapons and technology!

15) America became proud against the Lord **(Jer. 50:29d; 50:31; Jer.50:32a)**

16) It is the place where the nations gather. **The UN Headquarters is in NYC (Jer. 51:44c)**.

148

17) America like Rome also sits on 7 major mountain ranges - and it presently rides on (Rules over) the seven continents. It is the **head of nations** both militarily and economically (**Rev. 17:9**).

18) America was a Golden cup for the Lord because of its world missionary work, and it was blessed with great wealth (**Jer. 51:7a**)

19) America is Israel's sole protector, but according to prophecy we may betray that honor in the last days (**Isaiah 21:12; Jer. 51:24; Jer. 51:35-36**).

20) Isaiah 47:5 She shall no longer be called the lady of Kingdoms also referred to as a queen, for she is dethroned in one hour. (In Revelation she boasts "**I sit as a Queen**").

Isaiah 21:9 - "Babylon is fallen, is fallen." Interesting how it is repeated twice, not just in this passage but in **Rev. 14:8** and again in **Rev. 18:2.** Could this be a prophecy about the Twin Towers that fell on 9/11, one tower at a time? It could also prophecy that 9/11/2001 was just a warning/wake-up call before the major destruction that will occur during the apocalypse. The destruction of Babylon the great could also be the trigger point for the beginning of the great tribulation/apocalypse.

Isaiah 13: "And Babylon, the glory of kingdoms,

the beauty of the Chaldeans' pride, Will be as when God overthrew Sodom and Gomorrah."

Isaiah 47: "Therefore hear this now, *you who are* given to pleasures, Who dwell securely, Who say in your heart, 'I *am,* and *there is* no one else besides me; I shall not sit *as* a widow, Nor shall I know the loss of children'; But these two *things* shall come to you in a moment, in one day: The loss of children, and widowhood. They shall come upon you in their fullness Because of the multitude of your sorceries, for the great abundance of your enchantments."

In **Revelation 18**, Babylon the great is referred to as a "***great city***" that is destroyed in one hour. As just covered, I believe that as of 2014, **Revelation 18,** and **Jeremiah 50; and 51** are key chapters that eerily describe America. Unlike some bible scholars, I believe that the term "***Babylon the Great***" does not necessarily **only** refer to the end time world system and government that will reign during the apocalypse. I believe that Babylon the great may indeed be one great nation (great city) that will be destroyed. **Revelation 18**, is describing one nation because if it was relating to the whole world system, then who are these merchants that are standing at a distance observing a horrifying scene of massive destruction at one location? Here is the passage that identifies Babylon as a nation and not a system or religion:

Revelation 18:9-10

*"The kings of the earth who committed fornication and lived **luxuriously** with her will weep and lament for her, when they see the **smoke of her burning**, **standing at a distance for fear of her torment**, saying, 'Alas, alas, that **great city** Babylon, that mighty city! **For in one hour** your judgment has come.'*

As much as I wish it were not the case, as of this update America still perfectly fits the description of **Babylon the great** of **Rev. 18**. Could it be any other nation? Perhaps - but based on our current position and influence throughout the world - the USA is still the "head of nations".

Whether America aligns itself with the beast kingdom through some kind of pact, or is destroyed by the beast kingdom or some other entities, still remains to be seen. Please note that I am not trying to point a finger at the USA; the prophecies themselves point to the USA as Babylon the Great. Regardless, **every nation on earth** will be adversely affected during the apocalypse, not just America. ***If America fails or falls, the world as we know it will follow in short order***!

Regardless of its role at the very time of the end, whether victim or enabler the USA could be instrumental in forming the beast kingdom (whether intentionally or not); especially since it is still the most influential nation on earth. This is why certain characteristics of "Babylon the great" as described in the prophecies (read **Jeremiah 50 and 51, and Revelation 18**) so closely resemble America.

Unlike what happened in the prior world wars, Neither America, the EU, a one world government or any group of nations will be able to save the world during World War III (the Apocalypse). The prophecies are very clear about this; there is no interpreting or guessing necessary. In the end, God himself will have to step in to save the planet from total annihilation, cleanse the world of all its iniquity (**Revelation 16**), before Messiah can return (**Revelation 19; 20**)!

Revived Roman Empire, the European Union and its role during the Apocalypse

Some bible scholars believe that the Roman Empire re-emerges in the last days to become either **Babylon the Great** or the **beast kingdom**. They believe that Rome will re-emerge as part of a powerful united European Union in the last days. Other scholars believe that both entities are one in the same, and are thus representative of all kingdoms that exist at the time of the end.

This scenario does seem to fit somewhat with the prophecies of **Revelation 17**. However, it does not fit with **Revelation 18** because neither Rome nor the EU at this time is the leader of the west, nor the premier global superpower, or the richest nation on earth (which all describe Babylon the great).

As a result, if the EU evolves into the premier global power sometime from now to the time of the end, then it will more than likely be the beast nation under the control of the Antichrist described in **Revelation 17** instead of Babylon the Great described in **Rev. 18**.

The reason for this is that the description of the beast *with 7 heads and 10 horns* is more descriptive of a revived Roman empire which would be the aggressor/destroyer rather than Babylon the Great which will be destroyed. Under this scenario, the beast nation does destroy Babylon the Great as alluded to in the prior section and in the manner described in **Rev. 18**.

Another scenario is based on the supposition that the Roman Empire never really disappeared. It still exists today through all democratic nations that have incorporated the Roman form of government such as America and many other democratic nations that have structured its laws in accordance with the Treaty of Rome. So a **revived Roman Empire** has never really been such a stretch.

So in the later scenario, if we include America as a part of the revived Roman Empire/EU (since it is a member of NATO as well and also mutually referred to as "**the west**", then indeed the "great wealth" description of Babylon fits even better, and both **Revelation 17 and 18** would then perfectly describe such a powerful end time kingdom.

Another "remote" possibility would be that America might implode economically under its enormous debt loads thus allowing another nation, or group of nations such as the European Union to assume its position as the global and economic superpower at the time of the end. Given America's position in the world today (economically and militarily), I do not think this is a likely scenario.

So the point here is that it is all somewhat of a moving target, although the end time players are present and ready.

Why will Babylon the Great be Destroyed

Let me be clear that not just Babylon the great, but every single nation will be judged during the apocalypse. As the head of nations, one can surmise that the leader must bear the bulk of the blame. So let us list just a few transgressions on the part of the Babylon the great:
1) **Iniquity** was found in her and all the nations.
2) **Arrogant and Stubborn** - refusal to repent despite numerous judgments.
3) Although once Israel's protector - it became **Israel's Betrayer**
4) - A **land full of idols**. They glorify each other and not God.
5) According to **Jeremiah 51** - Babylon was a **golden cup** before the Lord; it had the word of God in her heart, but has fallen from grace.
6) **Abortion**. America led the abortion initiative throughout the world. America actually has compensated other countries for family planning - leading to over 1 billion abortions worldwide. **God must avenge the shedding of innocent.**
7) She is the **Pornography** leader of the world.
8) She is heavy into **Witchcraft and Astrology.**

I believe that the final straw for this great nation is her betrayal of Israel in the last days, especially since America was instrumental in brokering most if not all of the land for peace initiatives. You already know how God feels about this.

The USA sealed its fate when we chose to be the prime broker of peace agreements between Israel and its enemies which have pretty much forced Israel to surrender some of God's land for a peace that never materialized!

I believe that America had a unique calling to protect Israel given that is was formed as a Judeo-Christian nation. It was greatly blessed accordingly.
The following passages prophesy that America will betray Israel in the last days: **Lamentations 4:17; Joel 1:1-2; 17; Joel 2:20**
"Before your eyes I will repay Babylon and all who live in Babylonia for all the wrong they have done in Zion," declares the LORD." (**Jeremiah 51: 24**)

'The LORD has vindicated us; come, let us tell in Zion what the LORD our God has done.' (**Jeremiah 51: 10**)

"May the violence done to our flesh be upon Babylon," say the inhabitants of Zion. 'May our blood be on those who live in Babylonia,' says Jerusalem. Therefore, this is what the LORD says: 'See, I will defend your cause and avenge you'..." (**Jeremiah 51: 35-36**).

"Babylon must fall because of Israel's slain, just as the slain in all the earth have fallen because of Babylon" (**Jeremiah 51: 49**).

"A destroyer will come against Babylon; her warriors will be captured, and their bows will be broken. For the LORD is a God of retribution; he will repay in full." (**Jeremiah 51: 56**)

Isaiah and the writer of Psalm 137 also state how God will view the betrayal of Israel:

"O Daughter of Babylon, doomed to destruction, happy is he who repays you for what you have done to us" (**Psalm 137:8**)

"A dire vision has been shown to me: The traitor betrays, the looter takes loot. Elam, attack! Media, lay siege! I will bring to an end all the groaning she caused." (**Isaiah 21:2**)

"I will take vengeance; I will spare no one." (**Isaiah 47:3**)

All the nations of the world are equally guilty. The leaders of this lost world are more concerned about their selfish interests, climate change, and dividing up Israel's land (God's Land), instead of condemning terrorist acts, seeking the truth and justice.

Why such harsh Judgment?

A just God does not judge unfairly. Iniquity must be avenged in order to cleanse the land and eradicate evil from the earth. The earth must be cleansed before we can experience heaven on earth.

Who will destroy Babylon the Great?

As already discussed, we have strong indication from the bible that **Babylon the Great** will be a "**Western**" based nation (West of Israel), which I believe the prophecies point to America. It is still just a little too early to point fingers, but we know that three kingdoms (nation groups like the axis and allies of WW II) will form prior to the great tribulation.

The bible described them as the **kings of the North, East and South** (Daniel chapters 10, 11, and 12). Eerily the king of the West is not mentioned at all in the end time prophecies of **Revelation** and **Daniel**. I believe that it is because at the time of the end, the **king of the West, which is Babylon the great, will already have been destroyed.** The following verse lends credence to this belief:

Revelation 16:19

*"And the great city was divided into three parts, and the cities of the nations fell: and **Babylon the great** came in **remembrance before God**, to give unto her the cup of the wine of the fierceness of his wrath."*

Could the above passage reveal that at the time that all of the nations are punished, that God remembers Babylon the great because she already has been destroyed?

Of these three end-of-day kingdoms, the coming _**king of the North**_ nation or group of nations will be the prime perpetrator (as bible prophecy reveals). The king of the North may also host the antichrist, false prophet, and beast kingdom, or may be a key member nation of the ten heads of the beast!

The **book of Jeremiah** provides several important clues that the beast kingdom that destroys Babylon will come **from the North** (such as the **Medes** with perhaps the help of **Russia** or perhaps a **confederation** of nations led **by the Medes**). The Medes are the nations that include modern day Iran, Iraq, Syria. Let's read some passages:

Jeremiah 50:3
" For out of the north a nation comes up against her, which shall make her land desolate and no one shall dwell therein.
They shall move, they shall depart, both man and beast."

Jeremiah 50:23
" How the **hammer of the whole earth** has been cut apart and broken! How Babylon has become a **desolation** among the nations!

Jeremiah 50:41-42
"Behold, a people shall come **from the north**, and

*a great nation and many kings shall be raised up
from the ends of the earth.
They shall hold the bow and the lance;
they are cruel and shall not show mercy.
Their voice shall roar like the sea; they shall ride on
horses,
Set in array, like a man for the battle, against you,
O **daughter of Babylon**."----*

How will Babylon the Great be Destroyed?

She will be burned by fire: Revelation 17 and
18. Whether by Nuclear assault, asteroid impact or
volcanic eruption the prophecies reveal that she will
be destroyed by fire within one hour!
Could Rev. 8:12 be indicating that the 1/3rd of the
sun, moon, and stars being blackened may be
referring to a portion of the earth, the western
hemisphere being blackened due to a nuclear
attack on the west, including North America.
Isaiah 13, Joel 2:31

Jeremiah chapters 50 and 51 refer to end time
Babylon.

Jeremiah 50:8; 51:6; 51:45; Rev. 18 all are
repeated pleas from God for His people to flee from
Babylon. Contrary to popular Christian belief, the
latter tends to support those who believe that the
church will NOT be raptured prior to the tribulation
period, also referred to as the post tribulation
theory.

159

It will be a Global Judgment

Some people may think that the destruction of Babylon the great will be an isolated judgment and since they do not reside in that nation then as a result they will be safe. At first it may seem as such. Unfortunately, the prophecies do not align with that belief. The apocalypse will be a global event and as soon as Babylon is destroyed, the world will enter into an immediate severe depression couple with hyper-inflation as food supplies are rapidly depleted and rationed.

All nations will endure great tribulation; especially those that go after Israel during the battle of Armageddon. Notwithstanding, the last judgment consists of a massive global earthquake that will shake the very foundation of the entire earth; not just Babylon the great and the Middle East region. Many are in denial and think that some nations will escape the tribulation judgments. It will be a global judgment. Among many other passages **Isaiah 24** makes this very clear:

*"The **earth** is polluted because of its inhabitants, for they have transgressed the laws, violated the statutes, and broken the everlasting covenant.*
*Therefore **the curse devours the earth**, and its inhabitants are held guilty. Therefore **the inhabitants of the earth are burned**, and few men are left."* **Isaiah 24:5-6**

Chapter 11 - The Book of Daniel and the Apocalypse

It amazes me how much the book of Daniel contributes to our understanding of the book of Revelation, the end time events and their timeline. To coin a Perry Stone phrase "the book of Daniel concealed is the book of Revelation revealed"(8). In this chapter, you will discover why.

Both John and Daniel were in exile when they wrote their prophecies. Both saw the return of Messiah. Both escaped martyrdom and lived into their 90's. Both outlived their persecutors. Daniel was told to seal his visions, but John was not because Revelation was complete since the first coming of the Messiah had already come and gone before John wrote Revelation. Jesus death would unlock the prophecies of Daniel and Revelation! ***Daniel wrote for Israel - while John wrote for the church and Israel.***

The Giant Statue Image Made of Metals

Daniel and Revelation speak both of an empire with 10 horns (ten nations). In Daniel it is in the form of the 10 toes at the bottom of this giant statue image of a man composed of metals (**Dan. Ch. 2**) that king Nebuchadnezzar, the King of Babylon dreamed about.

This dream of an image of a giant statue (of a man made of distinct metals) was very prophetic as it described the major kingdoms that would succeed

Babylon through the remainder of this age; the age of man. Egypt and Assyria had already been defeated by Nebuchadnezzar of Babylon so four more kingdoms would succeed after Babylon, for a total of **_seven major kingdoms_** before the end of this age!

In king Nebuchadnezzar's dream, God revealed to Daniel (**Dan. 2:31-35**) the meaning of the different limbs of this statue as follows:

1) The **head of gold** is the Babylonian Empire
2) The **chest and arms of silver**: The Media-Persian empire.
3) The **belly and thighs of bronze**: Greek Empire
4) The **legs of iron**: Roman Empire. Like the two legs of the image, the Roman Empire was split in two divisions; the east and west.
5) Ten feet with ten toes of **iron mixed** with **clay**: is the beast kingdom that will rule in the last days.

Meaning of the last Kingdom of Iron mixed with Clay

*"Just as you saw that the feet and toes were partly of baked clay and partly of iron, so this will be **a divided kingdom**; yet it will have some of the strength of iron in it, even as you saw iron mixed with clay. As the toes were partly iron and partly clay, so this kingdom will be partly strong and partly brittle. And just as you saw the iron mixed with baked clay, so the people will be a mixture and will not remain united, any more than iron mixes with clay"* (**Daniel 2:41-43**).

Important Note: So from the above passage we now know that there will be two opposing empires (such as the West and Middle Eastern nations) or two opposing government systems (such as Democracy and Islam), and despite attempts at uniting them, just like the toes of the statue they just will not be able to mix. I believe this is why one of the systems (**Babylon the Great**) will be taken out so that the remaining beast kingdom can rule the world!

Meaning of the Stone that Collapses the Statue

The stone that crashes and collapses the image in **Daniel 2:34-35** is representative of ***Christ's second coming whereby all of the kingdoms on earth are destroyed***.

This lines up perfectly with what Jesus said in **Mathew 21:42** - "*The stone which the builders rejected has become the chief cornerstone*".

Jesus is the stone that topples the image in **Daniel 2:34-35!** We read of that actual event as a massive earthquake that destroys all of the nations at the moment or just before the Messiah returns in **Revelation 16:17-20**. We also read of a great stone falling from heaven that destroys the great city Babylon (**Rev. 18:21**), signifying Judgment by God in both cases. Let us explore the image of this giant man (**Dan. 2:31-45**) as it is one of the most important visions and prophecies in the bible

163

relative to the kingdoms of this earth past, present and future.

Regarding the image made of metals - Daniel Ch. 2

Let's review the meaning behind these metals that make up this image:
Head of gold: A symbol of Babylon. Babylon is a golden cup. This empire stole the gold from the Jewish temple. Babylon was an empire of gold, which possessed much gold, and made idols of gold, including the large 90 foot statue of Gold in **Daniel 3:1**. Just like gold represented old Babylon during Daniel's time, in the last days gold represents Babylon the great.

The two arms of silver: is a symbol of the Medes as they were famous for using silver as their monetary base, and to collect taxes.

Belly and thighs of bronze: is a symbol of the Greek Empire. Greece is synonymous with the Bronze Age, a period that lasted roughly three thousand years, and made Greece the center of activity in the Mediterranean.

The legs of iron: A symbol of the Roman Empire, whose military machine was fierce, ruthless and strong like iron. And as indicated previously, the Roman Empire was split in two divisions or legs; like the legs of the image.

Metal Symbols in the last days:

Feet of iron mixed with clay: The large metallic image in Daniel Ch. 2 had feet of iron mixed with clay and this last part of the image represents the last kingdom of this age. As Iron and clay do not mix well neither will the two dominant forms of governments in the last days; the West and Democracy versus the Islamic form of government, which are distrustful of each other.

Clay: Represents democracy. In the last days western influence and their style of resolving matters through diplomatic means will weaken and become ineffective. Just as clay is weak, the West will become more submissive and weaker at the time of the end. I believe that this is the reason why when the nations listed in **Ezekiel 38** invade Israel at the time of the end; the western nations that remain just sit back and ask why they are invading.

Iron: Represents Islam as their warriors are aggressive and fierce like the Roman Empire was. The former is known to behead their captives and whom they label as "infidels". They have no regard to the wives and children of their captives.

The prophecies indicate that their style of aggression and deception will get the upper hand at the time of the end.

The Tree Stump Vision of Daniel Ch. 4

This is another remarkable prophecy (**Dan. 4:10-37**). It is not only a dream and a warning to king Nebuchadnezzar of **ancient Babylon**, but dually it is a prophecy that applies to **Babylon the great** and the **beast kingdom** that reign at the time of the end!

The tree that was cut down was Nebuchadnezzar of **Babylon**. It was a symbol of the greatness that Nebuchadnezzar enjoyed (**Dan. 4:22**).

Babylon the great at the time of the end is also a symbol of greatness in these last days with its branches (it's influence) reaching to the end of the earth (**Rev.17:18**).

A watcher (an angel) shouts out loud to chop down the tree (**Dan. 4:14**).
In **Rev. 18:2** an angel shouts out "**Babylon the great is fallen, is Fallen**"!
The tree stump and roots were left intact to restore Nebuchadnezzar's kingdom if he repented (**Dan. 4:26**).

The Twin Towers were destroyed but America's foundation was not harmed in hopes that she repents in these Last days.

He was dethroned because of his arrogance (**Daniel 4:30**).
Babylon the Great will be destroyed because of her arrogance (**Rev. 18:7**).
Nebuchadnezzar was reduced to a beast for seven years.

The tribulation period will be seven years as well, with the "**beast**" kingdom reigning during the end times. By the way, the inhabitants of the earth who take the mark of the beast **_will all be reduced to beasts as well_** just as their leader of the beast kingdom, Satan.

In **Dan. 4:23** we learn that the tree was cut **but the stump had.....a band of Iron and Bronze.** This may be the key end time clue of who will form the beast empire. I believe this prophecy indicates that the beast kingdom will emerge from ten of the nations that comprised the old **Roman Empire** (Steel) and or the **Greek Empire** (Bronze) that the antichrist will establish one his headquarters in one of those nations.

The tree stump of Babylon being cut down also may be prophecy that although she does not exist as an empire any longer, the land of current day Iraq may be occupied by the head of the beast kingdom (the antichrist) at least at the onset of his kingdom **(Dan. 7:19; 23; Dan. 2:40; Dan. 7:7)**.

The **Roman Empire** was comprised of the following nations:

Israel, Jordan, **Syria**, **Lebanon**, Egypt, Libya, Morocco, Turkey, **Iraq**, Romania, Bulgaria, Germany, Britain, Spain, France, Italy, and Greece. The **Greek empire** was comprised of the following nations: Included Israel, Jordan, **Syria**, **Lebanon**, Egypt, Libya, Morocco, Turkey, **Iraq**, Romania,

Bulgaria, Germany, Greece, **Iran**, Afghanistan, Pakistan

All of the above gives clear indication that Muslim nations will form part of the ten nation end time beast kingdom **Dan 7:23-24;** the beast with seven heads and ten horns (**Rev. 13; 17).**

Note that **three of the 4 ancient empires** all ruled from the same HQ in ancient Babylon! Would perhaps the beast empire also rule out of modern day Babylon - Iraq? Interesting how the terror army ISIS in 2014 is currently trying to establish the headquarters for a united Islamic nation in Iraq!
So based on the above, the antichrist will emerge from a nation that was once within the conquered areas under the reign of the Roman and or Greek Empires.

We have already surmised that the **two rings** on the chopped down tree trump may be giving us the key clue that narrows it down to one or both of these two ancient empires. So based on this premise, the most likely areas are the following:

The antichrist will come out of which Nation?

Let's review possible candidate headquarters for the antichrist (ruler of the beast kingdom) and try to narrow it down...

Egypt: I do not believe he will emerge out of Egypt, since he will conquer Egypt, Libya and

Ethiopia.

Greece: is an economical wreck - not a military power or warring nation at this time. But the headquarters of the beast kingdom may emerge from one of the nations comprising the Greek Empire.

Rome: the antichrist could base from Rome if the EU becomes the beast kingdom, but not likely. Also, Muslim nations would never establish a headquarters at a non-Muslim nation - unless of course it took it over. However, as already noted the headquarters of the beast kingdom may emerge from one of the nations comprising the Roman and or Greek Empire.

Turkey: Turkey could be a strong possibility as the **headquarters of the beast kingdom**, especially if it merges with the Medes along with Assyria (read below) as part of the ten nation confederacy that will be part of the beast kingdom.

The Ottoman Empire was headquartered in Turkey, and was one of the longest lasting empires in history spanning 624 years from 1299 to 1923.

It ruled much of southeast Europe, Western Asia and North Africa. Its control over the Middle East was far greater than the Roman Empire. Some prophecy scholars believe that a *revived Ottoman Empire* at the time of the end may be the head of the ten nation beast kingdom prophesied in the books of Daniel and revelation.

Lending additional support to this theory is that the beast's army of **Ezekiel 38** identifies areas of modern day Turkey as the lead invaders. These areas listed include Magog, Meshech, and Tubal. Some believe Gog and Magog is Russia, and Russia may indeed also be a key force within the ten nation beast kingdom.

Finally, in **Revelation 2:13** Jesus reveals to us that the church at Pergamum is "***even where Satan's seat is...where Satan dwells***" Pergamum is located in modern day Turkey. So yes, Turkey may indeed be the host of the beast kingdom of the time of the end!

Medes: The prophecies indicate that the Medes, the area of **modern day Iran** will be a strong candidate, especially as one of the key forces within the ten nation coalition of the antichrist/beast kingdom. Current events and bible prophecies from Jeremiah, Daniel, Ezekiel and Revelation all indicate that the beast kingdom will emerge from the area of the Medes.

Assyria: This ***most likely*** is the area prophesied by the tree stump vision. This is the area of **Iraq, Lebanon, and Syria** - the old Babylonian empire territory! It fits the prophecy of being great to the east (of Israel), and South (of Israel).

Great to the East would encompass the nations of Iraq, **Iran (Medes)**, Afghanistan, and Pakistan. To the South would encompass the nations of Egypt,

Libya, and Ethiopia. Today, certain Muslim nations want a Caliph, an Iranian State where they all come together. As of 2014, ISIS is trying to create this united Islamic state.

Summary of the Tree Stump Prophecy

Based on all of the above, the tree stump that was left intact (**Dan. 4:26**),
will be the beast kingdom who destroys Babylon the Great (the great tree) in **Rev. 18**. They do this in order to attain total control of world affairs (**Rev. Ch. 13, 17**).

NOTE: Regarding the 7 heads of the beast of Revelation; these represent the major empires throughout History. Again the **number seven** comes to play, because it is **God's number of completion**! There will be no more man-made empires after the seventh - the age of man will cease after the seventh empire that reigns during the great tribulation!

So certain nations that comprised the Roman and Greek empires will form the ten nation beast kingdom that will engage in the turmoil and battles of the last days **Rev. 12:1-3**. These nations have crowns in Revelation because they are now individual nations during the apocalypse.

Based on the above, there is a strong possibility that the antichrist will establish his headquarters in the hotbed of an area that includes Iraq, and Syria. I also believe this because the River Euphrates runs through Iraq, and there are four very powerful and evil demonic forces (fallen angels) currently restrained in that area that will be released to afflict many during the apocalypse (**Rev. 9:14 and Rev. 16:12**)! Interesting how the cradle of civilization where this age started may be the headquarters of the last kingdom of the age of man.

A Sample of Satan's Meddling in the Spirit of Man and Nations

Why did a "Prince" of Satan attempt to stop Gabriel's final Visions for Daniel?
Satan the nemesis of mankind wants to keep us and the leaders of nations totally in the dark in these last days. Satan wants to keep us all both ignorant and enslaved; figuratively and literally.

This is why when God sent His messenger Gabriel to provide end time prophecies to Daniel, the angel encountered much resistance from Satan. This leads us to a very important event recorded in the book of Daniel.

The prince of the kingdom of Persia that withstood Gabriel for 21 days (**Daniel 10:12-13**) was a very powerful fallen angel of Satan, which is referred to as a **"prince"**. Satan has assigned certain powerful fallen angels to cause havoc and stir up strife in strategic regions of the globe.

Note: We learn in Revelation that four of these powerful evil entities are being held at the River Euphrates (area of Iraq), and will be released during the apocalypse to create even more havoc throughout the Mid-East region at the time of the end (**Rev. 9:14**)

The fact that Satan through his prince (fallen angel) did not want the Archangel Gabriel to give end of time visions to Daniel (**Daniel 10:12-21**), and also that the angel had to prompt Daniel to help him regain consciousness and be fully alert before the revelations were given, are indicative of the significance and importance of the revelations that Daniel was to record for **our generation.**

Most assuredly, the region of Persia, now modern day **Iran**, is a strategic area, and Satan most likely has one of his most powerful principalities assigned to this region. He wants to keep the pressure on God's Land and people **Israel**. Interesting how throughout history Persia/modern day Iran (and many of the surrounding Muslim nations), persist being Israel's greatest sworn enemies. It is an everlasting hatred that regrettably has no end; and most likely will lead the world - to the end.

You see, Satan wants all mankind to remain **ignorant** of the word and the truth. He wants to **keep mankind busy** with the worries and pleasures of life; and totally enslaved in bondage to Sin! This is why the prince (fallen angel) was directed to try to keep Gabriel from revealing the future evil schemes of the enemy, and the final outcome thereof!

The end time ruler appointed by Satan himself will be very cunning, just like his father the devil. This leader of the final beast kingdom will even wage war against God's people and God himself when he attempts to invade and destroy the Holy Land **(Daniel 11:45; Ezekiel 38:22-23; Revelation 12:17**). He will be destroyed not by the armies of man, but by God Himself (**Ezekiel 38:22; Revelation 20**).

Unfortunately, until Messiah returns Satan is not holding anything back since he knows that he is toast. Like a cornered tiger he is going to fight like crazy against God, His people and particularly against the return of the Messiah.

Revelation 12:12
*"Therefore rejoice ye heavens, and ye that dwell in them. **Woe** to the inhabitants of the earth and of the sea! For the devil is come down unto you, having great wrath, because he knows that he has but a short time."*

Chapter 12 - Ezekiel 38, Kings of North and South and the Apocalypse

Some scholars believe that Ezekiel 38 is a separate battle, and not the battle of Armageddon. On the other hand this may indeed be the battle of Armageddon (as I believe) for the following reasons:

1) The destruction will also come from God (**Ezekiel 38:22**)

2) There will also be a great earthquake (**Ezekiel 38:20**)

3) There will be a massive slaughter of the invading army (**Ezekiel 38:22; 39:12**)

4) The birds will be summoned to feast on the dead corpses (**Ezekiel 39:17**)

Certainly, there will probably be many wars and skirmishes during the apocalypse, but the battle of Armageddon will be the final battle of this age, occurring just before the return of the Lord.

The Middle East Battle of Gog and Magog is a war that is just over our horizon, yet was scheduled by God over 2500 years ago. In this war, the Russians (Gog, Magog), Ethiopians, Iranians, Turks, Libyans, and descendants of the Cushite peoples, will all come against Israel. Read about it in **Ezekiel 38:1-23**.

Why will certain nations want to invade Israel?

One reason may be that Israel is becoming the main source of reliable energy (natural gas) in the Mediterranean region. Through several failed enemy invasions Israel also has demonstrated that she is not a pushover and that the only way to possibly conquer her will be through a massive show of force, by nations willing to take massive casualty.

But I believe the main motive for an attack from its neighboring enemies is that everlasting hatred towards Israel. They may use many excuses for this invasion including Israel's alleged "occupation" of the Holy Land.

Among the several invaders listed in **Ezekiel 38**, is Gog/Magog, which many scholars believe is Russia. Even today, Russia is no ally of the USA. It vetoes pretty much all of our proposed sanctions against the Syrians, and Iranians. Recently the west has imposed severe sanctions against Russia for its invasion of Ukraine which are taking a heavy toll on Russia. Furthermore, Russia and China have both stated that they are completely opposed to military action by the United States against Iran and Syria, and they have even hinted that they would possibly even help defend those countries, against any action from the west.

Vladimir Putin had recently threatened the west by emphasizing that Russia has many nuclear weapons. Russia has probably the most plentiful stockpile of such weaponry on earth with over 5,000 warheads. They have raised the specter of nuclear war at least three times in the recent past as he and the West clash over the Ukraine conflict, which has been bringing to light other deep-seated animosity.

Falling world oil prices, due in part to fracking in North America, are devastating the Russian economy. While lowering our prices at the pump, one must wonder how Russia will react to an economic collapse in their country, and how much of their demise they will blame on the West. Could she eventually get desperate enough to kindle the flames that lead to **Ezekiel 38**?

Meanwhile, the Middle East remains in a state of chaos. According to one estimate, there are currently more than 20,000 missiles aimed at the nation of Israel. Some Israeli officials claim that Iran is even trying to develop a long-range missile capable of reaching the United States.

We don't know yet when this Ezekiel 38 invasion will take place, but I believe that once God wills it, it will happen quickly. Who knows, secret alliances and plans may already be in place and we will never know about it until it happens. It will take everybody by surprise.

Kings of the North and South

Although it was all in the future when the angel revealed what we know as the first 35 verses of **Daniel 11**, it's all history where we're concerned. But beginning in **Daniel 11:36** we fast forward to the time of the end when modern versions of these two kings will appear again and will ultimately oppose the anti-Christ.

I believe the current unrest in the Islamic Middle East, euphemistically called
The Arab Spring will soon result in the re-emergence of these two ancient
powers in a final contest for leadership of the Islamic world. Although the
players may be slightly different, it is still the same demonic spirit at work.

King of the North

Prophecies such as those in **Daniel 11:6-15** indicate that the antichrist's government (beast kingdom) will be headquartered among the "**King of the North**" group of nations. These prophecies indicate that it will be located most likely in one of the following nations: **Turkey, Syria, Iraq, and Iran**.

Today, Iran anxiously awaits the arrival on the scene of the Mahdi (the twelfth Imam) who will usher in a new age of "Peace", and the prophecies do indicate that Iran (the Medes) will play a significant role as a key member of the King of the North nations.

The **beast of Revelation 13:2** bears the symbol of a **Lion, Bear and leopard.** From a biblical perspective these animal symbols support the final Beast kingdom as being dominated by Muslim nations; including **Turkey** (the Leopard), **Iraq** (the Lion) and **Iran** (the Bear), among the ten nation coalition. Some consider **Russia** as representing the bear as it is also their national symbol. Indeed, **Russia (if it is Gog, Magog)** will be part of the invading force of **Ezekiel 38**, and may also be representative of the Medes (through alliance with Iran) which will form part of the ten nation beast kingdom. Other nations that may be a part of this ten nation confederacy may include **Libya, Egypt, Saudi Arabia, Syria, Jordan, and Ethiopia**.

As we have read **Turkey and Iran** are both prophesied to be among the invading force in the battle of Armageddon as described in **Ezekiel 38.** Now let's review Turkey as a candidate for the beast kingdom's headquarters.

Will Turkey be the King of the North's headquarters?

We already reviewed prophecies that indicate that the antichrist may establish his headquarters in **Iraq**. Now I want to indicate reasons and prophecies that support that his headquarters may be in **Turkey**.

Let me premise this by saying that when the biblical prophecies use terms such as beast, kingdom, king of the north, king of the south, etc. that it is usually referring to more than one nation or a specific area. So the headquarters of the beast kingdom is only important as a reference point; as the head of the beast - if you will. Also, the man of perdition may relocate his headquarters. In fact, the prophecies indicate that at the midpoint of the tribulation period the antichrist will relocate his headquarters to Jerusalem.

The Prime Minister of Turkey has made no secret of his belief that a **restored Ottoman Empire** will be the end times Caliphate. The area and peoples that **Daniel Ch. 11:6-15** refers to as the king of the north, is currently predominantly Muslim and spans the area of North Africa, the Middle East, the Arab peninsula, and Turkey. Coincidentally this is the area that the USA wants to get together militarily to deal with the threat of ISIS. So as you can see this whole area is in a volatile and chaotic state; a powder keg if you will desperately seeking a messianic like figure to organize and unite what the prime minister of Turkey defines as an *"**end time Caliphate**"*.

I believe that Israel will make the seven year peace treaty with the antichrist who at that time will reign from Turkey, Iraq or another of the nations comprising the final king of the north coalition.

This will be the trigger point of the tribulation period.

Recall that Turkey was the seat of the Eastern Roman Empire (Constantinople), during the later part of the Roman Empire, when it was split into western and eastern legs (the legs of iron of the statue in Daniel Ch. 2). In **Revelation 2:12-13** Jesus is telling us that the seat of power of Satan was in the area of Turkey at the time John wrote Revelation! **Let's read**:

"To the angel of the church in Pergamum write: 'I know your works, and where you dwell... **where Satan's throne is.** *And you hold fast to my name, and did not deny my faith even in the days in which Antipas was my faithful martyr, who was killed among you,* **where Satan dwells."** **Revelation 2:12-13**

So will the antichrist establish his future headquarters in the area near Pergamum, in Turkey? Strong possibility! Today, not much remains of the ancient city of Pergamum, but let's explore some more about what biblical prophecies refer to as the seat (the throne) of Satan!

Satan's Throne

As noted, Pergamum (an ancient city located in Turkey) was the center of pagan cults and influence in Asia Minor, and throughout the Roman Empire. Politically, it was the eastern leg of the Roman Empire. The city of Pergamum was devoted to the worship of many pagan gods.

During the time of the Roman Empire, Pergamum was the political headquarters which ruled all of Asia Minor under the authority of Rome.

It is called the dwelling place of Satan because of the gods that were worshipped in Pergamum. The residents at Pergamum were considered the temple keepers of Asia. The city featured three temples dedicated to the worship of three gods:

1) the Roman emperor,
2) the goddess Athena,
3) the altar of Zeus. The altar of Zeus is what is referred today as the throne of Satan.

The city also had a healing center called Asclepius (the Greek serpent god). They believed that Asclepius offered healing powers on those who believed in the serpent god Asclepius! The healing center was a major attraction in all of Asia Minor and many people including the Roman leaders and elite regularly visited the altars and the healing center. In order to preserve the image of supernatural power healing, patients that were **terminally ill** were not allowed to enter the healing center. Non-poisonous snakes that supposedly harnessed the healing power of Asclepius were used as part of the healing ritual. When the early Christians were sent to evangelize Pergamum, the cities pagan priests feared that the Christians would block the spiritual powers that they believed their gods possessed, and that thrived in their city. So the pagan priests complained to Rome that the spirits (demons) of their gods had appeared to them in dreams and warned them that the prayers of the Christians were driving their spirit out of the city!

So they went on the attack. They went first after Antipas. Antipas was a Christian Bishop appointed by the apostle John (author of Revelation). Antipas was ordered to make a sacrifice to a statue of the emperor, which of course Antipas refused. He was therefore sentenced to death at the altar of Zeus. Antipas was Martyred by being burned alive at the altar of Zeus. He was placed inside a hollow statue of a bronze bull atop the altar of Zeus, which was designed to function like a *makeshift crematory* for human sacrifice. Many centuries later this would be repeated at a much greater scale as we will now discover.

In 1864 the Germans excavated and later relocated the altar of Zeus to **Berlin, Germany**. It went on display at their Museums in 1930, just around the time that **Adolf Hitler** took power! At that time Albert Speer, chief architect for the Nazi party used the **Pergamum altar** as the model for the design of the grand stand were the masses would hail (worship) Hitler during the Nuremberg rallies and related Nazi party events. In a 1934 Nazi Party film which Hitler endorsed, he was represented as a Messiah like figure throughout the film.

Note: The Nuremburg rallies were held at night, with lighting effects (around 150 powerful search lights were used to light up the night sky). It was designed to create a mystical effect, as Hitler wanted it to feel like a religious experience; like a "Catholic mass" as he phrased it. The soldiers would also march around with torch lights adding to the mystical effects that Hitler desired. All designed to put the participants and audience in a trance like state. These theatrical rallies were called **"cathedral of lights"**, and was also used as the closing show at the conclusion of the 1934 Olympic Games in Berlin.

In **9/15/1935 Hitler** announced the **Nuremburg laws**. These were laws designed primarily to marginalize and strip the Jews of many of their rights and privileges as citizens. They were intentionally labeled as "subjects" in lieu of "citizens" of Germany. He used the term "final solution" at this speech.

In the Nuremberg adaptation of the Pergamum altar, the statue of the bronze bull atop the altar was replaced by the podium were Hitler would later announce his **final solution**, whereby he would orchestrate the burnt sacrifice of millions of innocent Jewish souls at the **crematories** of the **Nazi** death camps.

After the war Nazi chief architect Albert Speer said **"it is hard to recognize the devil when he has his hands on your shoulder"**.

Today, all that's left of the city of Pergamum, now in modern-day Turkey, are ruins.

So we learn in Rev 2:13 that the "seat of Satan" is located in Pergamum (Turkey - Istanbul).

When the **antichrist** steps onto the world scene, he'll appear to have all
of the solutions for **world peace**, enabling him to create a one world political, economic and religious system. He'll deceive many and will even establish a seven year treaty allowing Israel to build the third Temple and reinstate their worship of God there **(Daniel 9:27)**. However, within three and one half years (the midterm) of this treaty, as he solidifies world support he will claim himself to be God and eventually will lead many nations to the battle **Ezekiel 38** and **Armageddon** just before the Lord's return (**Rev 16:14-16**).

Will the Muslim Nations Unite?

As already noted the book of Daniel does seem to prophecy that the antichrist will emerge from one of the Muslim nations. As has been the case since ancient times, the Muslim nations have rarely been able to unite with each other and they will apparently resist the beast. **Daniel 11:40-45** may indicate that even among Islamic countries there will be resistance to the antichrist's rule, as other Islamic nations will also have their sights set on becoming the head of the coming world-wide caliphate.

Indeed, there has always been distrust and war between the Muslims, particularly between the Arab and non-Arab Muslims. But despite their disputes they have been known to unite to fight their true enemy Israel and the West, which they despise and refer to as "infidels". In the end the prophecies do indicate that they will unite at least for a short space of time to fight against Israel in the battle of Ezekiel 38 and the battle of Armageddon.

Also, in **Psalm 83:1-8** David prophesied that there will be a coming time (during the apocalypse) when all or most of Israel's enemies will finally unite in an effort to blot out "Israel" from the face of the earth (**Psalm 83:4**). We read: *"For they have consulted together with one consent; they are confederate against thee..."* (**Psalm 83:5**). .

According to these scriptures among the nations making up this confederation are:
"Edom [**Turkey**], and the Ishmaelites [**Saudi Arabia**]; Moab/Ammon [**Jordan**], and the Hagarenes [**Syria**]; Gebal [**Lebanon**], Amalek; the Philistines with the inhabitants of Tyre; Assur [their descendants migrated to **Germany**] is joined with them; they have helped the children of Lot" [again Moab and Ammon is modern Jordan]."

So the prophecies (**Daniel 11:40-43**) do indicate that at the time of the end the antichrist will succeed in uniting most if not all of the Muslim nations along with other non-Muslim nations, thus allowing him to eventually conquer Jerusalem, with little or no resistance from anyone, and making it his new headquarters for a short space of time. He will then put an end to the sacrifices at the rebuilt Jewish temple and erect an image of himself in its place. He will declare that he is god.

This will probably be the point where he requires that all worship him or face death.

In **Matt. 24:15** Jesus said the desecration of the Jewish temple with the image of the beast will be the primary cause of the *Great Tribulation*. This is because it will be the event that pits Satan and his man directly against God and His Anointed, Jesus Christ (**Psalm 2:2-3**).

The antichrist's defeat of Babylon the great, and the other opposing nations
could be the reason for the entire world to unite behind him declaring, "*Who is like the beast, w*ho can make war against him?*" (**Rev. 13:4**) And as Daniel was told, the antichrist will be successful until the time of wrath is completed because this is the way God has determined that it will happen (**Daniel 11:36, Revelation 17:17**).

**Current Events leading to the end time Kings of North and South
and Ezekiel 38**

In 2014, ten countries have formed a coalition against ISIS on the sidelines of the NATO summit in Wales: the **United States, U.K., Germany, France, Italy, Denmark, Poland, Turkey and Canada as well as non-NATO member Australia**. For those who believe the beast kingdom will be European, then this configuration could be the future ten nation beast kingdom configuration. But for reasons that I have already outlined, I do not believe that this is the ten nations of **Revelation 17:12-13** that will comprise the beast kingdom, as I believe that the ten nations of Revelation will include more Muslim nations than just Turkey.

I believe that the ten nations that comprise the **beast kingdom** will also be "**the King of the North coalition,** which is the group of nations that destroy **Babylon the great**".

The Bible tells of a coalition of Arabs and Turks called the '**king of the south**.' This King of the South will be militaristic, but this will end in disaster (**Daniel 11:40-43**). The USA is also attempting to encourage the rise of a durable Arab-Turkish confederation, and not just to combat the Islamic State. This may end up being prophetic, in that it could foment the final **King of the South** coalition!

If history is any guide we have learned that world wars sometimes grow out of local skirmishes or battles. Because of the ISIS threat, the United States has publicly pushed and supported the type of regional cooperation that could help lead to the formation of the biblical end time **King of the**

South of **Daniel 11:40-43.** So far, the formation that the west is supporting may include the following nations: **Saudi Arabia, Egypt, Turkey, Jordan, Bahrain, the United Arab Emirates, Kuwait, Oman and Qatar.**

I do not believe this is the final King of the South confederation, but the important point to notice is that agreements and alliances are already developing throughout the area that has been **"the battleground of history";** Europe, Asia, and the Middle East!

The final players of the beast kingdom, Kings of the North and South are
still fluid and work in progress. But I believe the final formation is already

planned and when God determines it is time, these alliances will form

relatively quickly, and will catch most by surprise. All it could take is one

worldwide calamity (man-made or not) to herald in the malignant beast kingdom; the one world government.

Many do not know where all of these coalitions will end up, but you and I already know that based on everything we have covered so far, the end time

alliance will eventually lead to a one world
government with **dire consequences** for all
mankind.

Chapter 13 - Left behind? What the prophecies reveal about the Rapture

The bible does give credence to a pre, mid and post-tribulation rapture scenario. Christian scholars have disagreed for centuries as to whether there will be a pre, mid or post-tribulation rapture. It seems that God has purposely planned it this way. Perhaps God does not want us in arrogance or pride to assume that we are automatically to be kept out of the tribulation period just because we "claim" to be saved or to be a "Christian". God searches the heart, and is not into labels. God also does not want our focus to be on when we will be raptured but rather on being ready at all times. He wants a relationship with us, through his son Jesus Christ so that we are indeed raptured on God's appointed time!

I understand that most pastors today teach that there will be a Pre-Tribulation rapture of the church and so no Christian will go through the apocalypse. I have some reservations about that because if Jesus and eleven of the twelve apostles where crucified and Martyred respectively, why does the church expect a special protection? Are we more righteous than the twelve apostles were? I also understand that God has not made it easy for us to figure it all out. He wants us to search out the truth - even if it takes a lifetime of work!

There are certain prophecies that make me feel that the rapture will occur sometime during the tribulation and I will present my case. But not to worry I will also present the scriptures that tend to support a Pre-Tribulation rapture.

The case for a Pre-Tribulation Rapture

In **Luke 21:34-23** Jesus said the following which infers that the church may be raptured prior to the day of the Lord's anger when He states the following:
*"But take heed to yourselves, lest your hearts be weighed down with carousing, drunkenness, and cares of this life, and that Day come on you unexpectedly. For it will come as a snare on all those who dwell on the face of the whole earth. Watch **therefore, and pray always that you may be counted worthy to escape** all these things that will come to pass, and to stand before the Son of Man."* **Luke 21:34-23 (NKJ)**

Some theologians believe that **Revelation Ch. 4** where we read that John is suddenly taken up to heaven, that this is proof of a pre-tribulation rapture. The rationale they use is that after chapter three the church is never mentioned again in the subsequent chapters of Revelation.

In Genesis 18-19: we learn that God did not totally destroy Sodom and Gomorrah until Lot was first removed. Lot represented the only righteous person in that whole society. However Lot was a relative of Abraham, so this is more an example of how God may spare the lives of whomever He wishes rather than an indication of a pre-tribulation rapture.

192

1 Thessalonians 5:9 assures us that God has not appointed us to wrath but to salvation through Jesus Christ.

Revelation 3:10 promises those who persevere that they will be kept from the hour of trial which will afflict the whole world.

The prophet Zephaniah brings this point home as well in the following passage:
*"Seek the Lord, all you humble of the earth, who have upheld His justice. Seek righteousness, seek humility. **Perhaps you may be sheltered on the day of the Lord's anger***." **Zephaniah 2:3**

We have just reviewed some passages that seem to affirm that there will be a pre-tribulation rapture. However, the book of Revelation makes it quite clear that many saints will be alive during the tribulation period (and many will be martyred). So we should all stay humble and pray not only for the unrepentant, but also for our own souls. Pray that the Lord finds us and our loved ones worthy to be sheltered on the "***day of the Lord's anger***" (**Zephaniah 2:3)**. Now let's review passages that support a mid and post-tribulation period.

Mid-Tribulation Rapture

Now let's review some passages that indicate that we may indeed **NOT** be raptured prior to the great tribulation.

In **Revelation 7:9 and 13-14** it is revealed that a great multitude of Christians will go through the Tribulation (this passage is cited below).
"After this I looked, and there was a great multitude that no one could count, from every nation, from all tribes and peoples and languages, standing before the throne and before the Lamb, robed in white, with palm branches in their hands."
Revelation 7:9

Granted that some will probably repent and accept Jesus as Lord and savior and will be saved during this period. However note what Jesus warns below in **Mathew 24:12** that many will not want to repent in the last days as their hearts will be hardened:

"And because lawlessness will abound, the love of many will grow cold." **Mathew 24:12**

The following passage reveals that a multitude of saints will endure great suffering during the tribulation. And their spirit will be completely shattered as prophesied as well in Daniel 12:7.

Revelation 7:13-14

*"Then one of the elders addressed me, saying, "Who are these, robed in white, and where have they come from?" I said to him, "Sir, you are the one that knows." Then he said to me, "**These are they who have come out of the great tribulation**; they **have washed their robes and made them white in the blood of the Lamb**."*

So we learn from the above that many saints will obviously endure great suffering during the tribulation.

Post-tribulation

Notice that the Bible shows that Jesus will return AFTER the tribulation, not before it:

"Immediately after the tribulation of those days the sun will be darkened, and the moon will not give its light; the stars will fall from heaven, and the powers of the heavens will be shaken. Then the sign of the Son of Man will appear in heaven, and then all the tribes of the earth will mourn, and they will see the Son of Man coming on the clouds of heaven with power and great glory. And He will send His angels with a great sound of a trumpet, and they will gather together His elect from the four winds, from one end of heaven to the other" **(Matthew 24:29-31).**

If the church is raptured, then who is the antichrist and Satan pursuing below during the apocalypse?

"And the dragon was enraged with the woman, and he went to make war with the rest of her offspring, who keep the commandments of God and have the testimony of Jesus Christ." **Revelation 12:17.**

1 Corinthians 15:51-55 discloses a mystery, and indicates that we will not all be asleep when we are caught up in the twinkling of an eye - in an instant.

But when we read this powerful message, we read in verse 52 that this event is to occur at the last trumpet, not before the first trumpet. This adds much credence to the **post tribulation theorists**.

Revelation 16:15 states "Behold I am coming as a thief...". This passage also lends credence to a ***post tribulation*** as it appears after the sixth bowl judgments near the end of the tribulation period.

Revelation 14:15-20 also gives indication of a post-tribulation rapture as an Angel is announcing the harvest of mankind after the trumpet judgments; near the end of the tribulation.

2 Peter 3:3-4 - *"Knowing this first, that there shall come in the last days scoffers, walking after their own lusts, and saying, where is the promise of his coming?"* This passage may lend more to a **post tribulation theory** since here scoffers are ridiculing believers about the return of the Lord, which apparently did not occur prior to the apocalypse.

Folks the Tribulation, if we can imagine, will be much worse than the Nazi death camps. The later was just a small taste of how horrible and terrible it will be during the day of the Lord's anger. I do however believe that even if we must go through the tribulation that sovereign God will shelter and protect those whom He wills. So ***Pray that He does shelter you during the apocalypse, and He may just do so***!

Regardless whether it is a pre, mid or post-tribulation rapture, we know for sure that we must be prepared for any scenario. So let us consecrate ourselves and commit our life to a relationship with our creator God in Jesus Christ, so that we may be found worthy to enter His kingdom at the appointed time.

In **1 Thessalonians 5:9-11** we are reassured in knowing that God did not appoint us to suffer wrath but to receive salvation through Jesus! So I would like to end this message on such a positive note.

"Watch therefore, and pray always, that ye may be accounted worthy to escape all these things that shall come to pass, and to stand before the Son of man" (**Luke. 21:35-38**).

Chapter 14 - How to Survive the Coming Apocalypse

I wanted to add this section just in case some of us are **left behind**! Does the bible say that we should prepare for the end of days? If so how should we prepare?

Should we prepare ourselves for a coming apocalypse?

Throughout the Bible there are ample examples of men of God preparing for an impending disaster during their life on earth. Some, such as Noah were specifically commanded by God to prepare. In Noah's case he was to build an ark in preparation for the great flood.

The proverbs (**Prov.27:12**) teach us that "a prudent man foresees evil and hides himself". We can begin the preparation process by first getting our spiritual house in order (**John 3:3**)

The scriptures teach us that there is a source for ultimate safety.
In Hebrew the word for safety is **Yeshua**. In English **Yeshua means Jesus**! During the apocalypse, just like today, our soul is and will become the only thing worth protecting and saving, since everything else will eventually be destroyed. Even if you manage to survive the apocalypse, one thing is for certain; all of us will eventually be destroyed upon our death, save our spirit!

The term "**prepper**" is given to anyone who is prepared or preparing him or herself from any potential calamity that has not yet occurred. Preppers vary widely on what they are preparing for. Some are deeply concerned about the potential for natural disasters and believe that we are now entering into a time when there will be catastrophic earth changes. Other preppers believe that terrorism is the most significant threat to our way of life. Government conspiracies, economic collapse, killer pandemics, EMP attack, World War III, martial law, solar mega-storms, asteroid strikes and societal chaos are just some of the potential threats that preppers are worried about. An economic collapse is one of the most common concerns for preppers.

As I already noted, throughout the Bible there are ample examples of men of God preparing for an impending disaster during their life on earth. The villagers in Noah's time laughed and mocked him and his family as they built this large ship in the middle of the desert. Even today if we heard of such a story we might laugh over how ridiculous it would be to build a ship in the desert. When the flood rains come, only Noah and his family survived the deluge.

We also read in **Genesis 41** how **Joseph, the son of Jacob** (Israel) was able to interpret the Egyptian Pharaoh's dream and thus Joseph was able to spare the Egypt and the surrounding nations from mass starvation by preparing during the seven bountiful years that preceded seven years of famine.

Abraham's relative Lot and his family had just one evening to prepare and evacuate **Sodom and Gomorrah** before that corrupted city was totally vaporized.

 So as our patriarchs prepared for the worse, we should also consider preparing for the seven year tribulation period.

Emergency Supplies

Storing emergency supplies is an essential first step. You may want to prepare an emergency kit that would include the following:

First Aid supplies
Canned foods
Ample water supplies, water purification systems
Power supplies: Batteries, Rechargeable batteries, flashlights, generator, fire starters, fire wood, solar panels
Communication: CB radio, two way radio,
Extra toiletries: Soap, TP, towels
Long Shelf life foods
Disposable utensils: Spoons, forks, knives, paper cups and plates
Outdoor Supplies: tent, sleeping bag, blankets, spare outdoor clothing, tools
Spare money: Cash and alternatives, gold, silver
Security: Night lights, Burglar alarm, Self defense (i.e. tear gas, etc.)

Garden: Grow an indoor or outdoor vegetable/fruit garden

Spiritual Food: Do NOT forget your Bible, faith and prayers for ultimate protection and survival! This is far more important than any of the other items!

Keep an extra kit of the above (including spiritual food) in the trunk of your car just in case any unforeseen event occurs that might force us to quickly force us to vacate our home.

Don't worry about being labeled a "prepper". Besides, no one should ever know about your emergency provisions, as these will become priceless commodities in a crisis situation, and if your neighbors know you have food or water in a protracted crisis situation, you and your family could face a life threatening security risk. Unlike Joseph, we do not have an entire army protecting our food stocks.

A military unit prepares for a battle by ensuring that they have an ample supply of food, water, ammo and shelter to survive a long campaign. Given all of the natural disasters that we have witnessed this past decade, we simply can't go wrong by being prepared.

How Do We Prepare Emotionally and Mentally:

Recognize that when we prepare ourselves against natural disasters wc are only protecting our temporary bodies which will eventually die off anyway. Recognize that we do not need to stock up on weapons nor build an underground bunker, nor take any other extravagant measures. These may actually just reflect - lack of faith!

In other words, being fully prepared for **eternal** life **is infinitely** (no pun intended) more important than earthly food, water and shelter. So let's prepare first in the following manners:

- We prepare by getting our spiritual life in order. We sharpen our knowledge in the word of God, and we pray regularly. We place our trust and faith in God, and not the things and treasures of this lost world.
- What will always work better than any man made arsenal or stockpile is the word of God, and a deep faith that the Lord will provide.

- "Trust in the LORD with all your heart; and lean not unto your own understanding. In all thy ways acknowledge him, and he shall direct thy paths" (**Proverbs 3:5-6).**
- **Jesus** said it best: "Lay not up for yourselves treasures upon earth, where moth and rust does corrupt, and where thieves break through and steal: but lay up for yourselves treasures in heaven, where neither moth nor rust doth corrupt, and where thieves do not break through nor steal" (**Matthew 6:19-20**).

- **We MUST put on the full armor of God...*Read Ephesians 6:11-18***

- **Claim the following blessing upon your life** when you choose to allow God in your life and to serve **Him who created you and the universe**:

*"**No weapon formed against you shall prosper**, and every tongue which rises against you in judgment you shall condemn. This is the heritage of the servants of the Lord, and their righteousness is from me," Says the Lord."* **Isaiah 54:17**

"Do not be anxious about anything, but in everything, by prayer and petition, with thanksgiving, present your requests to God. And the peace of God, which transcends all understanding, will guard your hearts and your minds in Christ Jesus"(**Phil. 4:6-7**).

Some Additional Preparation Tips:

- Convert a spare room or basement area into a long-term food storage pantry.

- Plant a survival garden.
- Install solar panel as a backup energy source and other alternative sources of energy.
- take a self-defense course.
- store 1 gallon per day for each household member.
- keep one (or more backpacks) filled with emergency supplies (Including toiletries, flashlight, batteries, emergency papers, cooking utensils,

radio, etc.).

- These emergency supplies should be near an exit door in case a rapid evacuation is required.
- Keep some clothing packed and ready to go in case you need to vacate your home in very short notice.

Survival Tips and Notes

- Get out of debt
- Gold and Silver will not be able to buy food so food will become priceless.
- Diversify away from paper assets
- Buy long shelf life food items as famine will become rampant
- Store plenty of water
- If you have land, learn to garden and how to can your foods
- Buy at outlets like Costco. At today's prices for around $300 you can buy enough food stuff to feed a person for one year.
- Purchase dehydrated or freeze dried or specially packaged foods that can last 20 years or so depending on storage conditions (the cooler the better).
- Buy non-perishables or foods that store well such as - rice, beans, oatmeal, canned foods, etc.

- **NOTE**: canned foods have been reported to also last much longer than the label advices (I am talking many years), especially if stored in a cool dry place.

You can search online for places to obtain long shelf life food stuffs, and also

for guidance on preparing, such as:

- Survival Blogs

- Prepper forums

- Prepper networks
- prepper website
- related search terms.

The point here is that you need to prepare and that it is relatively easy to do so. If you do not have sufficient assets to build large stock supplies, **this is one rare situation where I believe borrowing** and using credit to accumulate these assets is well worth it. After all, survival is priceless!

Below are some survival and long shelf life food sources:

Note: I am not personally recommending any of these sources. They are only a starting point for you to do your own research.

jimbakkershow.com/shop
nitro-pak.com
readymaderesources.com
911foodandwater.com
Beprepared.com
Lighthouseready.org

thrivelife.com/liveready
rei.com
first-aid-product.com
maxlifefoods.com
unclesamsretailoutlet.com
survivalmetrics.com
brownells.com
cheaperthandirt.com
majorsurplus.com
survivormall.com
chkadels.com
budk.com
survivalkitsonline.com
wildbillwholesale.com
thesurvivalplace.com
americansurvivalwholesale.com
sosproducts.com
wholesaleemergencysupplies.com

Search the following keywords:

Survival Blog
American Preppers Network
The Survival Mom
SHTFPlan.com
Prepper Website
Survival 4 Christians
Backdoor Survival
Off Grid Survival

I encourage all of you to consider maintaining an ample supply of food, water and other essential items to protect yourselves in the event of some natural, unnatural or supernatural event. It cannot hurt - it can only help. God forbid you ever need it, but if you ever do - you will be very happy that you have it on hand.

Overcoming Fear during the Apocalypse

Fear is one of Satan's most popular weapons. Hitler, Stalin, Cesar, terrorists and many other evil beings throughout this age have mastered this tool to control man. But when our spirit is nourished by the word and through communion with the Lord, fear is replaced with courage - the courage to persevere. We will be strong, knowing that the prince of this earth is no match to the God of heaven. Satan and his army of demons is no match for us, when we are equipped with the full armor of God. The Father, Son and Holy Ghost can make us indestructible and more importantly **incorruptible**! Let the following words from our Lord and the prophets reassure us:

"fear not them which kill the body, but are not able to kill the soul: but rather fear him which is able to destroy both soul and body in hell."
(**Matthew 10:28**).

"Yea, though I walk through the valley of the shadow of death, I will fear no evil: for thou art with me; thy rod and thy staff they comfort me..."
(***Psalm 23:4***).

John 14:6, *Jesus said, "I am the way and the truth and the life: no man comes unto the Father, but by me."*

"I make known the end from the beginning, from ancient times, what is still to come"(**Isaiah 46:10**).

Isaiah 48:6. *"You have heard all these things; look at them all. Will you not admit them? From now on I will tell you of new things, of hidden things unknown to you."*

"I know that you have little strength, yet you have kept my word and have not denied my name. Since you have kept my command to endure patiently, I will also keep you from the hour of trial that is going to come upon the whole world to test those who live on the earth." (**Rev. 3:8; 10**)

Chapter 15 - the Light at the end of the Tunnel

The purpose of this book is not just to help the reader identify events that alert us to the beginning of the seven year tribulation period. I trust that by now you are not concerned about exact dates, but rather something of much more value. It is to know where to find ultimate shelter, and to find the things that make for peace regardless of this chaotic world that is in the dawn of its destruction.

As we await the apocalypse, the wise person knows that all preparations can wait until we prepare our spiritual house. Once our spiritual house is in order, we will find peace, even in the chaotic world that we live in today.

As I write it is late December 2014, just a few days before New Year's Eve. I like many am somewhat apprehensive about what lies ahead in 2015 and beyond. If I were not a student of the word and the prophecies then perhaps I would understand why the world seems so oblivious to all of the storm signs starring at us over the horizon. But as a Christian I am full of hope, despite the evening news.

The end time prophecies should not depress us, but enlighten us to the glorious outcome that awaits those who persevere through the trials and tribulations of life. Do not shun the truth; rather embrace it so that you can experience the glory of the truth.

The world has become a land of many idols. I ponder at how so many people idolize sports figures and celebrities, and it reminds me how Samuel must have felt when the people of Israel rejected God as their king and demanded that God find them a man to become their king. How foolish for man to look to man for solutions and happiness. An honest look at the world news and world history leaves only one conclusion; without God first in our lives there is no hope for enduring peace or happiness.

Anytime we watch the evening news, we should be reminded of the depravity and fragility of life and how the apocalypse is not something far out in the future but rather something that can visit us in an instant. It is a searing reminder that whether young or old, healthy or terminally ill our number could be called instantly. Forget the rapture; tomorrow is not promised to anyone.
Like you, I do not want to go through the apocalypse. On the other hand we should not disregard the prophecies, and ignore the signs. The world today is in denial; it embellishes progress, and conceals iniquity. Alas, it is human nature to look on the bright side. The young want to experience more of the beauty of life, and the old want to guide and shelter their loved ones. Many are in denial and I understand why. But when we ignore the signs of the times we will be unprepared physically, spiritually and emotionally when the hammer drops.

"Most assuredly, I say to you, when you were younger, you girded yourself and walked where you wished; but when you are old, you will stretch out your hands, and another will gird you and carry you where you do not wish." **John 21:18**

In the prior verse, Jesus was telling the disciple Peter by what death Peter would glorify God. This message applies to all of God's elect who will be martyred for the glory of God during the apocalypse.

Just like the **sun is the center of our solar system**, and if it were not so **physical life** would not be possible, we must make the **son of God the center of our life** otherwise **eternal life** will not be possible. Just like the sun brings us warmth and light, as the world darkens with the approaching storm clouds of the apocalypse let Jesus be your guiding light.

Yes, there is a light at the end of this tunnel, and it is warmer and brighter than any light that we could imagine this side of heaven.
Godspeed!

*"Then Jesus spoke to them again, saying, "**I am the light of the world**. He who follows Me shall not walk in darkness, but have the light of life."*
John 8:12

If you found this book enlightening, would you please share this with others as follows:

1) Like our page at
https://www.facebook.com/RobertRiteBooks

2) Tweet "I recommend reading books @Robert Rite

3) Write a review on amazon.com or goodreads.com

4) Visit my blog that hosts many articles at: http://bible-blog.org

5) Consider reading my other books

Related Books by Robert Rite

- "Revelation Mysteries Decoded: Unlocking the Secrets of the coming Apocalypse"

- "Signs in the Heavens, Divine Secrets of the Zodiac & the Blood Moons of 2014!"

- "Apocalypse Codes - Decoding the Prophecies in the Book of Daniel"

- "Ancient Apocalypse Codes"

- "Aliens, Fallen Angels, Nephilim and the Supernatural"

- "Be healed!....How to Unlock the Supernatural Healing Power of God"

- "Awaken the Supernatural You!"

- "Blood Moons Rising"

- "Bible Verses for Supernatural Blessings"

    - "128 Powerful Bible Verses that can Save Your Life!"

Available at Amazon and other distribution channels

Resources and References:

1 - Seven Major Prophetic Signs Of The Second Coming - Commentary by Jack Kelley - gracethrufaith.com

2 - The End of America - Price, John (2013-09-11) - The Role of Islam in the End Times and Biblical Warnings to Flee America - Kindle Locations 6942-6969 Christian House Publishing, Inc. Kindle Edition.

3 - 15 'Signs of the Times' Indicating Judgment - Larry Tomczak -

4 - Understanding the Book of Revelation - by Dr. Ed Hindson

5 - The Mystery of the Shemitah - Cahn, Jonathan (2014-09-02)

6 - The Dark Side of Bible Prophecy - By Gary Stearman

7 - The Book of Daniel - Stendal, Russell (2012-05-01). (Closed Up and Sealed Until the Time of Fulfillment) LIFE SENTENCE Publishing.

8 - The Daniel Cipher - Perry Stone

9 - Global Surge of Great Earthquakes from 2004-2014 - newsroomamerica.com

22 - Babylon the Great is Fallen, is Fallen - Robert Rite

23 - Revelation Mysteries Decoded - Robert Rite

24 - Signs in the Heavens - Robert Rite

Printed in Great Britain
by Amazon.co.uk, Ltd.,
Marston Gate.